PENGUIN ANANDA
ETERNAL ECHOES

Yogi, mystic and visionary, Sadhguru is a spiritual master with a difference. Absolute clarity of perception places him in a unique space, not only in matters spiritual but in business, environmental and international affairs, and opens a new door on all that he touches.

Ranked amongst the fifty most influential people in India, Sadhguru is known as a speaker and opinion maker of international renown. He has been conferred the Padma Vibhushan, India's highest annual civilian award, accorded for exceptional and distinguished service.

Sadhguru has initiated large-scale ecological initiatives, such as Rally for Rivers and Cauvery Calling, to revitalize India's severely depleted rivers. These projects have found phenomenal support among India's people and leadership. They are internationally accredited and recognized as game changers that can establish a blueprint for global economic development that is ecologically sustainable.

Sadhguru has been a primary speaker at the United Nations General Assembly and several other UN forums. He has also been regularly invited to speak at establishments such as the World Economic Forum, the World Bank, the House of Lords, the University of Oxford, MIT, Google and Microsoft, to name a few.

With a celebratory engagement with life on all levels, Sadhguru's areas of active involvement encompass fields as diverse as architecture and visual design, poetry and painting, aviation and driving, sports and music. He is the designer of several unique buildings and consecrated spaces at the Isha Yoga Center, which have received wide attention for their combination of intense sacred power and strikingly innovative aesthetics.

Three decades ago, Sadhguru established the Isha Foundation, a non-profit human-service organization, with human wellbeing as its core commitment.

app.sadhguru.org
facebook.com/sadhguru
youtube.com/Sadhguru
rallyforrivers.org

isha.sadhguru.org
twitter.com/SadhguruJV
instagram.com/Sadhguru
cauverycalling.org

ETERNAL
ECHOES

A Book of Poems
1994–2021

SADHGURU

PENGUIN
ANANDA

An imprint of Penguin Random House

PENGUIN ANANDA

USA | Canada | UK | Ireland | Australia
New Zealand | India | South Africa | China

Penguin Ananda is part of the Penguin Random House group of companies
whose addresses can be found at global.penguinrandomhouse.com

Published by Penguin Random House India Pvt. Ltd
4th Floor, Capital Tower 1, MG Road,
Gurugram 122 002, Haryana, India

First published in Penguin Ananda by Penguin Random House India 2021

Copyright © Sadhguru 2021

ISBN 9780670096466

Font courtesy Isha Foundation

Printed at Thomson Press India Ltd, New Delhi

www.penguin.co.in

CONTENTS

LIFE

––––––––––– ••• –––––––––––

Time

DEATH

YOGA

GURU

MYSTICAL

• • •

Boundlessness/ Emptiness

TOIL

NATURE

• • •

Mountains

Rivers

SHIVA

EPIC

PEOPLE and PLACES

GRACE

---•••—————————————————•••—

A Note

Poetry is an in-between land between logic and magic. A terrain which allows you to explore and make meaning of the magical, but still have some kind of footing in logic.

When people experience something beautiful within themselves, the first urge is to burst forth into poetry. If you fall in love with someone, you start writing poetry because if you wrote in prose, it would feel stupid. You can only say logical things in prose, but you can say illogical things in poetry. To express all those dimensions of life which are beyond the logical, poetry is the only succor, as it is the language which allows you to go beyond the limitations of logic.

As a child and youth, my mind was so unstructured and untrained that I could never find a proper, logical, prose expression. Naturally, poetry became so much a part of my life.

My poetry first found a big spurt when I decided to start a farm. My farm was a very remote place, far from the city. I lived there alone for days, and sometimes weeks, on end without any contact with other human beings. At this time, I started writing poetry about pebbles, grasshoppers, blades of grass – just about anything. I found each one of them was a substantial subject to write about.

There was no power in the farm and around six o'clock in the evening it would get dark. I would stay awake till midnight, in almost six hours of total darkness. Somehow, I always found when your visual faculties are closed off, you naturally turn poetic. Maybe that is why we have heard of so many blind poets in the world. I am not saying that having sight should not evoke poetry – it has. But the nature of the human perception is such that it sees much more when the eyes do not see.

In about four months, during this dark period of the night in my farm, I wrote over 1600 poems. Unfortunately, none of these poems are with us today. I had written them on small sheets of paper that I found all over the place. I had kept a whole bunch in my car. Then there was a small fire accident where my car burned down and these poems got burnt.

The poems in this book are only what I have written in the last thirty years, since we moved to the Isha Yoga Center. I hope they find some resonance with you.

A poem is a piece of one's Heart, hope your heart beats with it and knows the rhythm of mine.

Much Love & Blessings,

Sadhguru

LIFE

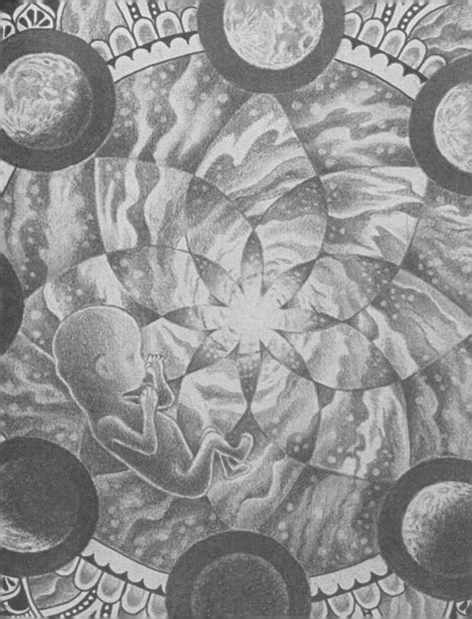

The Source

As the Cool Monsoon
breeze assuages the summer
burn like balm upon rash
Do you see the excitement in
the air of expectant leaves of
plant and tree stretching their
arms like long parted lovers
Ants scurrying around to close
and shore up their nests against
the oncoming deluge.
The peacocks have shifted their
conversation from contentedness of
summer's warmth to concern of
preserving their magnificent
but oversized plumes.
Farmers preparing their tools to
plough and overturn the richness
of the soil with the very first showers.
The city folks preparing their long
forgotten umbrellas and in some cities
maybe their boats
All the excitement is only of
life finding life. Perpetuating
life by the dictates of its
Source

———•••••———

Life is a Drama
You have to play.
Must also know
when to come off stage.

———•••••———

Many images of life
Linger for ever, an album
Of all that has been. Thanx
To technology without speaking
A word we may share our albums

Mingle

Ah' the joy of knowing
that your very body
shall become the green
leaf and the red flower

Over time there shall be
no visceral evidence of
One's earthly venture
The very sod that we
walk upon are us

Every leaf and flower
are us. Only in Spirit
can you know this
Mingle. In this Mingle
is the essence of all that is life.

Life

The cool mountain breeze
Caresses me and the mountains
Cold, bare and blue
These ageless brooding rocks
Much life they have
Sustained, nourished and snuffed out

In your bosom you have borne
Men of gentle love and heartless treachery
Many a man has spilt blood
Upon you by accident or intent

The cool mountain breeze caresses me
Inviting to life and death.

Fall time...

In Life and in Death
the sweetest of all
of mother earth's breast.
As the leaves so shall we...

————·····————

In Life
In Death
To Know
Is All

————····●————

Life an easy ride
if no concern of how and where
destination is guaranteed
and no fare.

Frenzy

I claim these Dry leaves
are mine and of course the
Blue sky, as all else has
been claimed. Insufficiency
of one's existence makes Humans
claim all that they set their
eyes upon. Land, Soil, Water
People and even patches of Moon.

Lunar scape is going through
property division, if this is not
Lunatic what else. In longing
to Belong and in turn possess
This brief life of Birth and Death
has turned into a Fanatical
Frenzy.

Transform

In the shifting sands of time
The powerful and the powerless
need each other to wrestle life's
many formulations. No one really
comes on top as all shall perish.
But the essence is not in Rise
or Fall. Did you sing a
canorous tune or are you a
cacophony of bitterness, regret
and shame. Life is not a Race
to be adjudged at the finish line.
But a breeze that can touch and
Transform

Insight

Flights of fancy will take us
not to destinations afar
Nor dead logic carry us
through terrains unknown

It is not the planets nor
the lines upon one's brow
But one's ability to see

See all that most fail to see
Insight into within and without
That allows life to achieve flight

——— ••••• ———

Life is a dream
But the dream is true

Now that it is your dream
You must make it happen.

——— ••••• ———

Life is life...

Life is not about fame
life is not about wealth
life is just about Life
life is all that we have.
Rest is all an illusion.
Life is Life

When...

When...
A Man is Woman
Bird a Flower
Red is Blue
Life – Death
Twilight

———·····———

Fool

A fool is a fool
being too full and
unable to receive or
perceive and hence a fool.

To be a fool is not cool
But everybody is somebody's
Fool

Passage

The bees and gnats did flowers seek
But man that claims to be in His image
Spends his life burying trinkets in vastness vast
Trinkets of men and women of children and wealth
The eyes set upon trinkets in greed and attachment
Can see not the pure pleasure of life and beyond
Come awake and alive to life
Arise into the life within and life without
Life and life is the only passage to yonder and beyond

Peace

War and war
the in-between space, we call the peace

Peace, peace only
in preparation for another war

On principles we have fought
for boundaries we are fighting still

In the name of god
many a slaughter we have performed

Filling this graceful planet
with the odious smell of anger and hate

Oh, slumbering ones, come let us dissolve
the blood-thirsting monster within us

Here, drink from the fragrance of my being
and know the bliss of living

Uyir Nokkam (Life's Purpose)

Only if you experience, I exist
If you become unaware, I cease to exist.

Only in the Blossoming of life does your god exist
When grace blossoms, are you not the god.

You were soil, now become flower
One who was human becomes the soil

For flowers and plants, roots are the source
For your life to blossom, I am the Source.

Why does life need gold or wealth
Only purpose of life is life itself

Only purpose of life is life and life within

A purpose that is innocent of Desire and Anger
A purpose that is bereft of Attachment and Sin
The purpose that fills you with love and bliss is
Just the life within

Only when the life within blossoms, you attain liberation

Let the thorns of a flower be seen
By those with an eye for flowers:
Not by those who harvest
Thorns

In body we may be
Man, Woman, Tree, Bird
Insect or a Worm. In life
We are just One life.

Dissolving Together

Being together is the beginning
Working together is the middle
Dissolving together is the ULTIMATE.

———•••••———

Life has come from a very beautiful source.
If you remain in touch with that source,
everything about you will be beautiful.

HOOKED

Scent of a flower
Coolness of a breezy whiff
The celestial splendor of the
Night. Relentless beat of the
Heart and gentle movement
of Breath. All these seemingly
innocuous happenings make
Me a living, throbbing, intense
life. This Brilliant mix of
innocuous and the Incredible
can only be an outcome
of a Mindless, unthinking
Intelligence of the Beyond.
That made me a slave
in my own life. A life
without persona, a life
bereft of its own longings
A life that is conquered
by the Infinite will
The cool fire of this eternal mill
burns me not but leaves me
Blissed out and Hooked

Garment

The weave, the texture, the colour
all this and more has enamoured
the hand and the eye. The unclean eye
sees garment as a barrier
for its lust and longings. Yes.
The hand of the Maker has
woven your body to a finesse
that the dyers, weavers and connoisseurs
can never conceive. The Body beautiful,
why shroud it with Garment

Lost in the skills of the Maker
May you not miss the Maker.
Body the Masterpiece is an abode of
Ah the Selfish One. The Only One.

Being

All trees shaking
their heads
saying yes nor no

It is the breeze that
moves them
and they
move the breeze

Isn't this the way
for you and
Shambho too

Life affair

A passion with You
You and You. Unbridled
Passion for all and everything
An Unconstipated life and love
Making life a love affair
Beyond needs and desires
That make life a breeze
Or a scream as you wish
Will you Ride the phenomenon
of life or wear yourself
down with endless longing

Nomadic lust

Of Roads and endless roads
of wheels that roll wearing
themselves down to transport
us to quench our nomadic lust.
Forests, Plains, Deserts, Mountains
and Oceanside all in a blur
but imprinted, etched to
change our lives with richness
of this earth's wealth of visual
Delights and climatic wonders
Nomadic lust shall forever
keep you from Insanity
of turning Humans into
Heaps of Things

Leela

To know the Profound Playfully
If only you had a Joyful Mind
A Heart with overflowing Love
A Burning Intensity in your Body
You would be playful with
Life and Death
Matters of Here and Hereafter.

——— • • • • • ———

Of work and relaxation
Of rest and work out
Golfing is no goofing.
Play, play life, or just be a goof.

Frisbee

If you are willing to play,
a piece of plastic could be your way.

———·····———

When life is in full throttle
Above all, do not wobble.

Skill Thrill

A Ball can be hit, spun, wrung around,
bent. All subject to your attention that
can make the inanimate come Alive!

———•••••———

A ball should roll
A basket hold
A ball in a basket
Well, it is a racket
Hence, a basket with a hole

———•••••———

A ball can change the world.

Adventure

When pangs of passion arise
for dimensions that are of
no personal concern begins
the Adventure of life. What a
croaking toad you should be
to invest life into transactions
of ventures of exchange. Adventure
not a conquest but a surrender
of Oneself to something that
has no return on investment

Of Giving and Living

Saw a flower thought it was giving
On a closer look realized it is only living
Giving an idea sprouted in the minds
Of those succumbed to cerebral complex
Holding concepts as virtue over living
Living not an idea but a boundless real
Giving and taking transactions of petty minds
Living is the only grandeur that will endure
Test of time and stretch of timeless

Is All just a striving to sustain the living
In becoming just the living is the fruition
Of all life within and without
Shall we abandon and deny the cosmic
Deny living to nurture a conceptual comic
This not of giving and living but living and living
Living not as a process of acquiring and hoarding
Living as life can only be, just a throb
That leaves no distinction betwixt common and cosmic

Life full of waves of many sort.
If you Ride it, it is a possibility.
Problem if crushed by the same.

Every bridge crossed
is another possibility
realized. Peril of life
unlived, is in uncrossed bridges.

—— ••••• ——

Life is in its context
Set a context of love and
Everyone turns into an Angel
In hate all shall turn into Devils
Frame yourself in the right
Context and be the King of your life.

—— ••••• ——

Unless you stake your life,
Life will not be won

Awards

Will someone award the
lovely blossom that brings
colour and cheer to the spring.
Will someone reward the Honey
bee for his meticulous toil
of accumulating sweetness from
sources you could not imagine.

Well most disregard the Beauty
Of the Blossom and raid the
Bounty of the humble Bee.

Subtle Graces and the Sweetness
are rewards of the highest order

Here - Yes Here

Born of bodily fluids
guaranteed of an earthly end
Promises of heaven have turned
mortal men into immortal menace.
Those who made up eternal
life will not value the bit
of life that is here and Now.

Life here distorted by promises
of hereafter. Just for you to
know, those who don't make
it here shall not make it anywhere

It is Here and Here that
the Hereafter is hidden.

Heavens...

Secrets of life slithered
in the form of a Serpent.
For becoming the Agent of life
the serpent got all the flak from
the falsehood of otherworldly creed
who made the very flesh we live in
a mortal sin. They invented
worlds that none ever visited
as the sacred and only through the
most corrupt of men can you get there.
Is there a greater crime than denying
life here, to be had elsewhere.

Stri

In ignorance of Lord's abode
found an alternate in mother's womb

The generation to come is only the bounty
of the womb and the breast

Sanctity of which man has lost
to make it all a play of lust

One who does not revere the space of his creation
will inevitably lend himself to oblivion

Within and without there is a woman
the glory of life is hidden in celebrating this woman

Pain

My pain is not of the wounded
nor is this the pain of the lost
nor of defeat and failure

This is the pain of the mother
when the one in her womb
turned against her

She would be willing to go
just to let him be
If she lets go she will kill,
this is the pain of knowing

In your love you will destroy
in your withdrawal you will destroy
that which is but your part

Till the part is willing to be whole
the pain will take its toll
This true of creation and me

Chant - Glory

Incessant chant to break bonds
Croaking of a frog to make bonds
All seem similar to an Eye-ignorant

Both of course longing to fulfill
One longings of his loins
Another longing to fulfill
a longing that is not even
their own but thirst
of life to find its Innate
Glory

Unformed

Just born fish knows to swim
A bird inevitably learns to fly
A dog shall bark no matter what...
Humans come so unformed
that growing into a Human is
an arduous project – ask your parents
Life unformed means finishing
has been left to you to form
to your pleasure or wisdom.
All that you are can be improved
constantly till the last day.
Don't you forget the first day
you had to be turned upside down
and a tight slap upon your
backside even to get you to breathe.
Unformed is Unlimited Possibility

Destiny

Destiny is not a done thing
it is a string that makes
a garland of flower, bead or bone

You may wear it now or later
here or there. Or you may
place it upon the bosom of another

But even a flower shall not fall
without the tug of the string

———•••••———

A child is someone who is
fresh from the Divine works.

Try not to teach but imbibe
the ways of the Divine.

———•••••———

A child's dream to capture
It is not just about a picture
Capture you wish to, all that
You can see and can not.

Child is a reminder
of your beginnings

In your beginning is the way
to the Beyond.

Among children
to be a child

The masks of adulthood
If entangled, shall be gruesome.

The Sparkle

The Sparkle in this child's eye
Should not die as we turned a blind eye.

We should confront the divisive lie
Lost life cannot be mourned with an empty sigh.

For the sake of lives lost and lives yet to be made
Let us at least have the courage to call spade a spade.

The sparkle in this child's eye
Let the warmth in our hearts see that it does not die.

A child is Born

A child is born
not unto a purpose of his own
nor to fulfill parental agendas.

A child is born
Not to bring pain nor pleasure
nor to foist misery nor joy.

A child is born
Not to serve a cause or a mission
nor to conquer or surrender.

A child is born
A phenomenon unto himself
As a cause and consequence of life.

As all life longing to be full
To blossom and to Perish
A child is born

Forsaken

A Human is born alone
though held in the innards of
one's own flesh.
Alone he forms himself
Alone he blunders through life.

The possible Oneness, at every step
he tramples, missing the Oneness
of the spirit and flesh
Forsaking the glory of going
beyond one's own cerebral mess

The hapless orphan lives
alone & dies alone.

The gracious few who are of the
Oneness of life & beyond are mocked
as fools of empty fortune.

Yes – you have a Dream

Childhood full of Dreams
of climbing a Tree or hill
or of flying off to moon or mars

Adolescence is lucid in its
Dreams and pangs of groin
and heart, of love & lust
Driven by the body's juices

Adulthood is troubled with
Dreams of success and fears of
failure. Of money, wealth and
possession that seem to enhance life.
Dreams of children and their
children, of their glories and
achievements that could deliver
you beyond where yours stopped.

When shall you stop Dreaming
and sink your roots into
the creation and its Source.
Or this life forever Dream it shall remain.
Yes – you have a Dream

In these Dreams being
unfulfilled you shall feel
like a fool but in fulfilment
An Utter Fool

ageless

Of age and agelessness
age is of the body and
agelessness is a matter of spirit.

Those stuck in biological tangle
wish for eternal youthfulness.
When one wants to stop aging
Is it about infantile inadequacies
or of compulsions of adolescence
or maturity of middle age.
Well, does no one value ripeness
of wisdom, the privilege of the Aged.

Fragility of the infant, freshness
of adolescence, a measured approach
of the middle ages. Above all
ripeness of spirit, where it is
not about the sweet flesh
nor the smooth skin but only
about the spiritual seed.

Though all have their place
and time. In the blossoming
of the Being lies the beauty of
Life

Blossoming

The glory of sunrise
happens, the blessed moon
grows full, the sweet blossoming
of the flowers happen not
with any brazen announcement
or attendant music.

The Universe an expression
of geometry perfect. All that is
misaligned will perish without
reaching fullness. It is in alignment
with all that is, that this Being
can Blossom to the fullest.
Blossoming of an individual
too happens quietly, gently
unannounced without din
or drama like all things
of Significance.

A Day. A Life

The birds tweet
of something sweet

There is no lofty intent
in this conversational content

It is all about a grain or an insect
or of the day's meteorological prospect

Of tweeting, tumbling, breeding
till Death are you content doing?

Chopper

The can that flies
carries me through
the space above my
mother and my bond – Terra (BHUMAA)
leaving me in a state of
utter freedom and danger
leaving me free to court
Life, Love or Death.

life

The most Restless Ones
Rest so well when life is
taken out of them.
As if the only Curse was
life.

———••••• ———

Come quite a distance
But birth and death are
not the events that matter
Eventful life you must aspire

Action

In being free from the need for Action,
Shall one know the Joy of Action.
Intense Action without intent.
Pure Action Pure Bliss.

———•••••———

A dream is what's on your mind
Work is what's at hand.

Sounds of Life

Speech is of the society.
Words are of the mind.
Sounds are of nature.
The soundless is of the beyond.
Thus if One gets identified by one's own speech,
that One will belong to the society.
If One gets identified with one's words,
that One will belong to the mind.
If one gets identified with one's sounds,
that one will belong to nature.

If one dissolves in the soundless silence,
then to that one alone the realms of the beyond will yield -
to that one alone.

Carbon Life

Piece of coal that
burns into ashes, with
right amount of striving
can turn into Diamond
Stable and Brilliant
Lest you go unshining
The carbon life that you are
Sheer Stability could make you
Forever.

———•••••———

The wisdom of the old
Freshness and energy
Of the young life, is ideal
Recipe for life's blossoming

———•••••———

The juice of life is in detail
Bereft of detail deflated life entails

———•••••———

Food has to be good.
Not just for the tongue
But for body and being.

An Ode to Coffee

As a seed does not
reveal the shape of the tree
The innocence of the infant face
does not reveal the sage or the sorcerer to come

The white beauty of a blossom with
The fragrance to rival the majestic jasmine
Does not reveal the enslaving
Insane concoction of your beans

Half the world has surrendered to you
The other half are either ignorant of your
Magic or have turned ascetic and
Refused to succumb to you
Of all of man's ingenuity in
Extracting pleasure and nourishment
From the Mother earth's breast
You stand out to be the one
to inspire a fierce faith
Of unquenchable sort

You have overshadowed the lord of light
As for the faithful Daybreak means you and not the sun

My Little Finger

Enough of this false poetry.
I break my pen to see that
none of it ever spills upon paper.

But the green leaf sings its green poems
and the brown one, about to lose its
perch upon the tree, murmurs its own.
The bird upon the tree sets music
to its own kind.
The insects are ardent singers
of their own 'bardery' and even the
toads echo with their grave verse.

My heart has a mind of its own
and sings away against my resolve.

Now can my little finger
be left behind.

The Fall

The Fall of the leaf
Is but the enrichment of the sod
Life giving nourishment for
worm, insects, tree, bird and animal
O' Man when shall you learn
that life shall flourish not by leaving
no stone unturned but in letting
all life be as they are.
The Fallen shall rise in their time

Recycle

As I crush the fragile snow in my step
to expose the brooding blackness of the soil

The countless men that walked
upon this life-sustaining soil
to be sucked in by this dark soil in life recycle
seem to creep up my feet and claim
everything that I thought as me
as a part of themselves

All that is me is just a segment
in the continuum of eternal recycle

Having lost the joy of not knowing
but soaked in the blissful heaviness of knowing
I plod on, exposing ancestral pain
and sprightly spring in silent waiting

Me continuing to expose
the brooding darkness of the soil
with every step being a continuum
of the eternal Recycle

To Be, to Breathe...

They say a new year has arrived
but the Sun feels the same to me
The clouds are the same unreliable forms,
The Moon continues to play the blushing bride
of showing herself in wax and wane.
Am I missing something!
I squat to touch the ever reliable
Terra firma, a fistful of wet sod.
It all feels the same.
Then I close my eyes as it is the
nature of my tribe to close eyes
when we really wish to see.

Ah' now I see I am lighter by a year.
As the burden of years peel off
I am lighter of the years gone by.
The exhilaration of being closer
to the Destination, the joy of
the journey multiplies.

To Be, to Breathe is Bliss.

Time

the day...

the day is but a piece
of Time. Time the stage
upon which drama of
substance and space plays.
To make you know the beauty
of the play, knowing the
feel of the stage a must.
Without having feel of the day
the play of sunlight, breeze
breath, love, laughter
life as you know is dubiously
fragile. To be anxious, tense,
insecure and having fear
lurking behind the next
corner is but natural to
One who has no feel of the stage
A Day

Circa 2020

Doors closed, windows open
Wistful, fearful but hopeful eyes
scanning for the invisible
elusive virus or its carriers
Unseen and shrouded in its minuteness
the One who has brought the world
to its knees Dances on. When the judicious
ones are being judged as cowards
and the very bold are Dead.

Quack solutions are a plenty.
Not knowing the nature of this
miniscule visitor Humanity in Quandary.
Humbling – brings out the Best
and the Worst from different sorts

A challenge of Our Times

Who Rides

Who Rides and who gets
Crushed are matters of
Times. Lives made
and Unmade not
always of Good vs Bad

——— ••••• ———

a day is but a piece of time
that lets us live and die.
this day let us live
and live totally.

Money Matters

Money Matters O' Man
are not just a bleed

But eating into the very Marrow
of you, me and Mother Earth

You are selling your marrow
in hope of a better tomorrow

Tomorrow a day that never
comes is eating your Today

Today the Only Day
To Live and to Die

Tomorrow

A day that never came
but has managed to spoil every game
One day that takes all the blame,
the basis of all fear and shame

Cripples the blossoming of life's flame
A spoiler that makes life a dream
Traps the limitless in a limited scene
A day that never comes
but the world it rules.
Tomorrow

Preserve We Must

Preserve we must,
not for being remembered
but with the hope and Blessing
that the posterity is enriched.

The future is awoken
by the intensity of the present
and the wisdom of the past
It is in these times Three
Is rooted the eternal tree.

There is no new or old
for one who is in a timeless mode.

Ho Ho Ho

The year is coming to a close
And what have you done this year?
One more year gone.
Are you still alive?
And what are you alive to? And what are you dead to?
When was the last time you saw a full moon?
Or a sun rise?
When was the last time you gazed at a mountain or the ocean?
Or looked at a butterfly fly?
When was the last time you saw a flower blossom?
Or kicked a ball?
When was the last time you smiled at yourself?
When was the last time you looked back and could laugh at yourself?
For the last few days of the year and for the years to come, get into the act and make it happen for yourself.

A year gone by

In the year gone by
have you let life bypass you
Have you let the joy of your being
find expression or have you
found reasons to excuse yourself
Have you let the love in your heart
warm this world or have you found
reasonable excuse to languish in frown
Did you find something wonderful
to say of all around you or have you
become the judgment day damnation
Have you loved, laughed and teared up
or have you remained untouched by life
Years shall go by

Timespace

Years pass by
bodies born and die
people cry and laugh
some love and hate
Ruthless time rolls on
without a footprint
in the scape of Timespace
Happy New Year

———•••••———

You may Laugh or Cry
You may Dance or Crawl
The sands of time
Shall continue to flow Mercifully.

———•••••———

Time is timeless
Age is ageless
If you are egoless
And joyfully guileless

My Day is Taken

My day does not belong
to Me. Today is My day
but does not belong to Me.
Yesterday, Today and the
Next day do not belong to Me.
Yes My day is taken to
unveil the most obvious,
as most are oblivious of
the Beautiful nature of
Being Human. The
boundaries of the Body have brought
bondage to the Being.
Knowing the Being that
we are, is all there is to see.
Yes My day is taken.

In the seamless journey of time
Ignorance attempts to frame life
As past, Present, and future
The Timeless One's relevance is not framed.

The dials of time
mime the planetary rhyme

Gets everyone on the run
In all this there is a Still-One.

DEATH

My Day

A lonely Buzzard sits
upon a tree at my window.
He looks at me with interest
seems disappointed that I am
a bit too Alive. He wants me
or someone or something to die.
But he looks like an icon
of Patience. The limits of His Patience is the
length of lease of life that
we have. I say to him
I shall not keep you in waiting
forever nor will it be too soon

You shall have your Day
But, This is my Day

All Shall Pass

The clock tic tocks
My life away, relentless
And ruthless. Driving me
towards my designated
Goal, not of Glory but Grave.
Grave it shall be for all
The Honored and the Humbled
Shall all make it to one goal
Bound or unbound, in
misery or joy, the Brave
and the Beaten all shall
enjoin in the earthy embrace
But the benediction of
Creation is such that not
One shall fail. As all
Shall pass

No Trace

There is no Container Service
for those who depart but still
most have turned their Homes
into warehouses. How fortunate that
nothing can be taken even by the most
ambitious. If they could, by now they
would have weighed the heavens down
well below all that we know. As the years
roll on without leaving a trace of themselves.
Only humans desperately cling to their
memories and count and recount them
as years. Just to remind themselves that
they too lived.

Do not be too proud

When you live do not be too proud of things
that you possess, 'cause
when you die all that you get is a stone.

———•••••———

At the End of Our Journey

As at the end of our journey
There is no final
Resting place
Then we need not fear
Losing our way.

EMBRACE

In the end a man shall lay
Upon the bosom of mother earth
The only one who is always in waiting
Unconditional
Willing to take you whole
Bone and flesh
Blood and brain
Fluids and filth
All shall find
Unconditional embrace.

Let it Rattle

I would know
you are happy
if your bones did Smile
and I hear the rattle.
Not the cackle of an old witch
nor that of an infant.
But the gentle smile of the
flower, fruit and leaf. The smile
of plains, mountains and rivers.
The absorbing smile of the
ocean, earth and moon.
Let me see, feel and hear
the smiles of your bones.
Before the maggots eat through your marrow...

Inertia

Inertia of the un-prompt
Inertia of the unenthusiastic
Inertia of the uncaring
Inertia of the unloving
Will miss the effervescence of life
Life is just the overflow of the
Effervescent source of creation

Inertia is an invite to Death
Inertia is the process of becoming inert.
Inertia in attitude and practice
Is about establishing rigor mortis
In Installments.

Effervescence

Effervescence of nectar seeking bird
Effervescence of a truant school boy
Effervescence of a stung Romeo
Effervescence of fish, flower and fiend

Beyond good and evil there is life
To live and to know life and deeper life
Is touched only by the effervescent

The effervescent one will transcend
the Inertia of Death.
Deathless is he who knows
Effervescence without purpose.

.......before he creeps up on you.

Deepest crevices of the body
Where the life-making magic
is rooted and effulgent.
In the very same crevices
is the dark depth pregnant
with inertia of Death.

To be upon the highest pitch
One needs to constantly enliven.
To be ahead of the Sun in coming
Awake. To be alive enough to
Welcome the Moon and the Stars.
To imbibe the fragrance of the
Flower ahead of the bees and the Birds.
To know the coolness of the
Mist before it touches the Leaf or a
Blade of grass. To be able to catch a
Snowflake in its journey of descent.

To know the stillness of Death
before He creeps up on You

———•••••———

The Deathless Stillness if you fear
Your own well-being will you impair.

———•••••———

The measure of your growth
Is a truth you will have to face
To partake in life upon this earth
Or to face the consequence of death

———•••••———

The sacred wheel
Has lost its axle
You and me have to toil
Before we meet the soil

a pitcher, a pot

Potter's hands pluck the flesh
of the earth to knead and mold.
Does he know he is kneading
his own flesh to form another
body to hold water or milk.

A pitcher, a pot, a body, an earth
flesh of flesh, soil of soil
The potter who kneads will be kneaded too.

The Mother's knead, you should neither
fear nor impede. This magical
deed could render you as
sweetness of a mango or the flighty
feather upon an eagle's wing
or maybe a scholar or a king
a pitcher or a pot

Devdasi

Mortal nature of this coil
Is earth's gift, but only soil
Hosts and breathes like an anthill
Prances and dances as if of its own will
If life's mill has kneaded you well

Will know a destiny beyond death's will
One who escapes the death's cold chill
Will succumb to the ultimate thrill
To be enclosed in a timeless still
This, the spiritual whore calls Divine Will

Dancer

Death defying rattle
of the Drum, the Ash
Smeared Yogi wild
with the fire of destruction
playing out the role of
The Enlightened. Not in
pursuit of gods above
or the juice of life and its
pleasures did he Dance.
Dance not celebrating the
life of flesh but permanence
and finality of Ash the only
Residual of all that lives
Fierce Dancer – not to
entertain but to Enlighten

Fall Time

The Fall of a leaf so gentle
But profound, as those
who fall willingly are the
Ones to rise to the highest
The colorful glee is a death dance
Many glories of the life cycle.

Death Divine

Unmaking of life as you know it
is the dark dimension of death

Only in unmaking life as you know it
will render you to the ways of the Divine

Ways of the Divine strange as it may seem
are true workings of reality

Reality is not true as you know it
but to know it as it IS
is in letting yourself soak
in the mortal nature of who you are

Life as you know it
is but a deception
a dodging of the Divine

Death
Death of life as you know it
is Divine.

Misty Magic

Misty magic of the mountain dew
Drops so fragile and resilient
Drops hanging from the tips of leaves,
drops rolling down the blades of grass
Drops that linger upon the spider's web
like a jewel of many splendored diamonds
Indestructible in its fragility
Beautiful as only a Trap can be.
Trap for the poor insect but palace
for the majestic spider crafting a
Cosmos of dexterity that decides
the fates of many lowly creatures
that are food and play for the
majestic spider with his many legs
and his spindle craft. The disdain
that he spills for the two legged
cripples as he dances upon his
agile 8 legs casting inviting
nets of Hope and Death.
Death of the living who pity the Dead
Not knowing the bondage of life and freedom
of Death.

The Only striving worth its name is to strive for death from which there is no resurrection. A Death so complete that it frees you of the need to exist. When you are free from the need to spin webs that are cast to trap. One who traps cannot leave the web either, trapped into his own trap.

Without setting a trap there is neither work, food nor play. So the trap has to be crafted with one's heart strings of love, pain and ecstasy.

Décor not of diamonds but drops of ecstasy that only those steeped in love can smell. A trap that drips with juices of life that flood away the fears of death. Such an overflow of life that defies death and touches the Beyond Here and Now. Such a honey trap when you shake, drops of life will fall not unto Death but into the Beyond.

Misty Magic (*Cont.*)

Veils of misty myopia
Cocoon one with the warmth
of blindness beautiful
The beauty of a leaf, flower,
light, shadow, breast, hair
The myopic mist makes it all fair
You may burn your way
through these veils of mist
Or
O'Beloved trust me
Behold my spirit in your Heart
Hold my hand in love
Become an ecstatic drip
That will let you flow unto the Beyond.

Beings of the Beyond

The ruthless debtor that she is
claimed back earth that you fancied was you
To leave you so naked and bare as to be bodiless
dead they think you are when you wait for another lease

Since earth's debt you repaid
ones who claimed to love you abhor you
With me the wanderer of the twilight world
you can rest upon my breast,
to annul your destined course.

Death

Life and death live in me at once
Never held one above the other
When one stands far, life I offer
In closeness, only death I deal
In death of the limited
Will the deathless be
How to tell the fools
Of my taintless evil.

Living Death

As the gurgling
Mountain brook wove its
way through the mist filled
slopes and steeps, the sounds
of the elemental sort blowing
vibrant tunes in the innards
of my energetic self.
The tingle of the formless
aqua taking the forms of
molecules and cells, neurons
and viscera, blood and bones
leaves me quaking
in throes of nameless ecstasies
It lets me live Death
wiping out all lines that could
tell me what is me and what is Not

YOGA

Mukthi

A Strange drift. Overwhelming
All that I knew, all that I
always was, all that I ever wanted
to be, all that meant something to me
Not at all unpleasant but a sense
of Sweetness of being
soaked in sugar syrup
A drowning and death of one
and conception and birth of another
A familiar me being dissolved
An unfamiliar power being born
Seemed like a catastrophe
Catastrophe for the puny me
An effulgent Celebration
for the Life as it exploded beyond
the limits of my body and perceptions.
Having been a prisoner
of my own device
Feel embarrassed to celebrate
Liberation

The Only Bondage

You did escape the trap
of elemental hive.

But it is your own doing
that is the ultimate trap

Till you go beyond your own crap
there is no way to break this trap.

————•••••————

Seeker's Predicament

From muses and mystics you did hear
Seeming to be the sounds of phantom lands

In ignorance's bind, life, like phantom seems
Oh, creatures of surface, the depths of life will you ever seek.

Cosmic Stuff

It is a common fact
We are all cosmic stuff
Fabricated in such
Uncommon flair and taste.

In not realizing the original state
We could lay this limitless fortune
Into a hapless cosmic waste.

The cosmic so chaste
Maybe nothing is a waste
But don't you want a taste
Of its eternal Estate.

Snails

On inward journey
Humanity moves
Greasy tracks
Like mud snails they make

Snails are good
Only in French recipes

Even the garlic
In extreme concentration
Could move them not

When on journey to
Immeasurable land
Move you should
Like a furious snake
Snail you choose
For gastronomic needs
For your spiritual need
Choose a lightning steed

endless longing

If you do not know
the pain of fullness
what are you...
In trying to please
all and sundry, end up
croaking like a lonely toad.
Believe the make believe
and be lost in endless
longing...

Body's Plight

This toy of elemental ploy
Deceptive in its ability for joy
The pain and bondage of these miraculous five
If broken, you in liberation will fly.

———•••••———

The mischief of elements five
Did make this marvelous hive
Not only to endure the journey
But to know the sweetness of honey.

———·····———

Sweetness sucked from the soil
drips through the blessed fruit.

To reap the sweet sap of the mortal coil
look not for the Fruit but the Root.

———·····———

Bonding

The Body Bonds with all
that touches it. Mind
a fickle friend but
the Body solid in every
Sense. Every Bond a Sacred
Connection to Mother-Earth

Helicopter

Two blades chopping
thin air. Chuk chuk chuk

Do you understand the
gravity of the situation.

You have beaten the Gravity
that causes the earthly bondage.

A force that no human
mind has been able to decipher.

A force that makes you feel like
a crawling creature.

Or is this the force of
Mother Earth's loving embrace.

Is she holding you
to her loving bosom.

Or is she reminding you
that what you think as 'ME'
has to mingle with her mud.

Is this a motherly intent
of love and possession.

Or is it a murderous
intent of making you
mud and manure.

Chuk chuk chuk

Moments of being free
from all this and more.

Perspective

Of the green leaf
and the brown leaf

The difference is of
the earth and the sky

Of the earth and the sky
Difference there is not

O' humans, look the earth
is in the sky. Only perspective.

———•••••———

Camera can capture
life as a caricature
Only spirited you
can know the life spirit.

———•••••———

Bull Could Pull

If you harness right
Even your Bull could pull
With the rope and the yoke
You could do your Masterstroke

Search

It is the stench of manure
that enchants you
as the fragrance of a flower
It is the excreta that you abhor
that you relish
in the sweetness of fruit
It is this body of flesh and bone
that cuts
the temple stone
Are you searching for Shambho

Curiosity

Empty Sky is potent
but shy. Limitless possibility
held in a deceptive haze
Is this Divine ploy
Or Nature acting coy

Open in every way
Nowhere to go and no way
Bondage wrapped in freedom
Everything floating in nothing
Nothing in everything
Absolute chaos but order
most perfect. Would you
think you could know all
this, with mere curiosity

Human

Even when at Home
I longed for Home

Searing pain of longing for Home
strangely got cured in being Homeless
when the walls of Home dissolved
A Pristine Home unwalled and
unfettered, devoid of love
affection or companions blossomed

Shall I call it My Being.

Yoga

Your face is hard,
they think you are a loveless wench
To me you are like a lover's song
gentle as the spring breeze
Like a mango tree in full bloom
every leaf hides a delicious fruit

Such bare and scarce ways
did your progenitor describe you:
folks would never know
the luscious lass that you are

Clothed in rough and common raiment,
who could dream
of the uncommon possibility
that you are

I espied and pursued you
with a stout heart

Waiting and wooing
for lifetimes three

Trailing you through terrain unknown
of untold pain and sweetness too
The very journey has left me so complete—
the creation and creator are within me

Can no more see the world without you

Cosmic Drop

A Drop that cleared
Illusions of this and that
Here and There, of me and you
A Drop that obliterated
Small and Big – Divine and Devil
A Drop that fused forever
The Eternal and Momentary
Raising the vision beyond the two

The Drop that turned me inside out
The Drop that tore distinction of Body-Soul
The Drop that enslaved me to become itself
The Drop that is me, longing to become you
The Drop my heart calls Shambho

Yogic Lore
here comes to the fore
Wisdom more ancient than mountain
exists here beyond scriptural mention.

The science of Yoga is a Ladder
to the Divine. Go up or down
lands you in the same place. It is
a choice you make.

BEING

The meaningless journey
of life, urges you to hanker
for movement, as to stagnate
is death. To go and keep
going. But where is there to
go. When all that is, is here
within me. When time and space
are illusions of ignorance. When
the shadow of life is mistaken for life.
In measuring the length and breadth
of shadow is about crystalizing
one's ignorance. It is not about
where to go or how far to go.
Going far is a manifestation
of life steeped in ignorance.
The question is not even about
to go or not to go. In relinquishing
the non-existent journey
shall you know the Bliss of Being

...Of Meanings

Call it what you want
Love, Friendship, Purpose
or God. You are scanning
the invisible for an
Illusion that may assist
your life, to find meaning.

In Abandoning this search
shall you find the Invisible
Presence sans meaning.
To ride this great phenomenon
of Creation without Contamination
of Meanings

Divine Hand

As I see the seemingly
perpetual play of breath

The breath: the maker of my body,
The taker of my being
When the timely moment comes

This ceaseless play
of the unseen hand
of the Divine

Me firmly held the hand
And the maker could not escape.

Gnana

The Breath
The Body
The Being
The Bonding
The bondage
a misunderstanding

~ 18 Feb 2011
Samyama
Day III

Samyama

The Madness of Mantra
this mad ecstasy
could break the deepest bonds
of within and without
when even the body could contain me no more

The cool awareness of the breath
Oh, this breath my bondage and my Mukthi.

How deep it goes into me!
Tickles the tiny bond with this body
This blessed breath the cause of life
is the gateway for life beyond

Taste this breath of life enhancing venom
This same breath I've tasted for ages
If this deadly venom can take us to celestial heights
Isn't every atom a door to Heaven?
Is there a musician to play
for the Dance unbounded?

Treachery

My Breath
My Dear Breath
Of all the treacherous Beings
I have known and believed
To be mine or a part of Me.
As life matured realized
that none were mine or my part
But you My Dear Breath
Me thought but my inseparable part
But here today you reveal your
Ultimate treachery that you
neither mine nor my part.
But instead of being broken
As by treacherous acts of many.
Here I lay Alone, untouched,
Blissedout

————•••••————

Fresh breath
Fresh life
Life and death
All in one breath

————•••••————

Trees

What they exhale
We inhale
We may live bereft of friendship
But our lives are laced in this relationship

A Brief

In the beat of a heart
In the gentle passage of
a breath. In the intermittence
of pulse. Does life
happen and so does
Death.
A fleeting moment embodies
the dynamism of Creation
and stillness of its Source

My Bounty

With eyes open the
Beauty of an extravagant
Creation. When my eyes
close the profound Intensity
of the Source. To open or close
A choice that is no choice
My Bounty

Shoonya

The translucent seeming light
lays me bare
The turmoil of the existence around
and my inner stillness
Is this Man, Beast or God
They must wonder
Tear drops border my eyes
not of love, joy or pain
But of all-encompassing Stillness.

———•••••———

You don't have to do anything,
you don't have to think anything,
you don't have to feel anything to be complete.
You are complete by yourself.

———•••••———

The Still One finds
little company.
Stillness, an Action without purpose
is not just a repose.

———•••••———

The pulse of our lives
is in the many offering
of Mother Earth. Grains
grams, legumes and pulses

———•••••———

Between rest and activity
there is a porous net.
When committed to wellbeing of All
activity percolates into the rest.
But none can take away my restfulness.

Cosmic Dancer

There is no Dance
Without a Dancer

The Dancer is not felt
In Dance perfect

The perfection of the Dance
Dissolves the Dancer into the Dance

Reveling in the Dance
One may miss the Dancer

Absolute attention to the Dance
Will bring forth the Dancer effulgent

Only in knowing the Dancer
All the Dance is revealed

The speed, the rhythm and the flight
Are all just the Dancer's sleight

Colourless

The exuberance of colour
in sunrises and sunsets,
in leaf and flower, in rainbows
and shadows. All the play
of colourless light! In touching
the hueless Being, shall
become capable of every nuance
of colour. The myriad impressions
of this colourful universe just
the leela (play) of the hueless Being
Vairagya (beyond colour)

light plain...

In breaking light plain,
the seven hues did not complain
Broke the binding vow
into this enchanting bow
Seven within and you know
only in a supplicating bow

————·····————

All creatures of the world
are an expression of the Creator.
If you are willing, every creature
is a doorway to the Creator.

Here and Here

These people want to know who I am,
these children of God
drunk upon the fruit of ignorance
want to know where I come from

These pearly dewdrops that
hang precariously from the blades of grass
I'm in them

The lovely fresh orange blossom of the spring
I'm in them

The silent songs of these timeless rocks
I'm in that

The age-old scent of the cedars
I'm in that

The sweetness that the
mother's breast bares for the child
I'm in that

The coyotes howling away in their ancient sorrows
I'm in that

Where is there for me to come from
Where is there to go

All has become stillness as everything that's moving and
unmoving is me

My Yoga

Lost all sense about Sounds
and Silence. In utter Chaos
am in absolute Balance. Excruciating
Pain enjoined with profound Pleasure.
The Grief of losing a loved one also
brings the gravitas of Stillness. In a
world where the leaf cannot
know the Sweetness of the accompanying
fruit nor the Fragrance of the flower
that it spawns. Here I am
tasting the very source at
the surface. Lost all sense
of the sacred and sacrilegious.

O' Shambho, since I embraced you
a Speck on the periphery seems to be
the very Center. Valleys have turned
into Peaks. What should have
been utter Confusion has become Crystal Clarity.

I am a Man with a man
A Woman with a woman
A creature with a creature
A Goblin among goblins
Just know with you I am
You.

What shall I do

What shall I do with this Myself
Which is all and nothing at once
What shall I do with this Myself
Which is me and you at once
What shall I do

——•••••——

Transformation

One dimension of Yoga is to stretch
yourself to the limits. As it is only in
touching your limits will you have the true
desire to Transcend. Transcendence the
only Transformation.

Muscles

Oh, these muscles like
serpents entwine my bone
and should say the vital all.

Though they cannot even
stand by themselves
We can twist, turn, hop and jump
Not without these no mean
muscles. My muscles are
my Play, my Dance, my
postures Yogic, my muscles are
my barometer to tell me when
I've gone too far. Of all the
Wonderful things the pain that has
preserved me from self-destruction
Is most profound. These radars
of pain and pleasure telling me
what to do and what not to do

In being flexible you can
fit into anything and be what
you want – Yoga Yoga.

Above all Balance
You can unleash Human Potential
Only when in perfect Balance

Balance

Control is not Balance.
Balance is ultimate Control.

Reflection

No one ever denied
me anything I need.
As I never asked nor
expected anything from anyone.
All that I ever could want
was within.

As I soaked in the world
Its beauty, its nuances
its light, its sounds and smells
Aching joys of love and its lustre
Saw all only in
Reflection

...Unintended

A flower blossoms with
no intent, all who have a
nose for fragrance shall
enjoy this unintended
Permeation of Pleasure.

A fruit ripens not to
give us sweetness but
just a sweet packaging
of its seed. The seed
that has the potential
to make the whole Earth green.

May you blossom to your
fullest, not to serve or sacrifice
but fulfilling life's longing
for itself. A Blossoming of
your Being shall bring
Unintended Blessedness to All.

GURU

Lap of Master

There are peaks of awareness
and Valleys of Grace

At the peaks one shall
know the brilliance of knowing

In the valleys you can
melt into the mist of Oneness

Masters lap a melting pot
of brilliance and grace, of knowing
and dissolving. It is a place
to pray, play or perish.

Pray – You shall be graced with much
Play – You shall know Bliss of Being
Perish – You shall become One with him.

A Cloud of Substance

The formless fluffy cloud
you pass through, and feel
that it is not of much substance
This formless mass of little substance
is the bearer of life-giving rain
in its absence all would be vain

Your Master's presence is not
a substance that you can touch in vain,
but for parched hearts,
in devotion, there is copious rain

Blessed are those who know
the nourishment of the Master's lap

Blessed are those who soak
in the shower of Grace

Guru

The moth, to shed its
dreary life of darkness seeks firelight
for warmth and light

As it circumambulates in flight
it is filled with light and might

When being around light
becomes too much delight,
wants to plunge straight
into this light delight

Then thinks, when me am
willing to burn in him,
he stands straight
to be bright

And the flame speaks:
O ye of meager flight!

Yet to know, burning bright,
it is me that burns through the night

waiting for a moth of meager flight
to make him bright and light

———•••••———

A Guru is someone who
dispels the darkness
in you. You can call him
a light bulb if you want.

———•••••———

A Rock is an easy prey
for the Guru. A Rock can
be brought into the ways
of the Divine without hammer or chisel
Just a touch and he reverberates forever.

Stones You can break
With the hammer strike
How to pierce open human
Hearts and Heads.

Yes, I have found a way

Disarm

Sit still says my heart
Do not raise your dust
Let the world find its way to you
But my mind, the worldly wise says
Raise a storm
or you'll never get this world to disarm

My Bond

My bond for you is of light
and not just of love,
let me soak your body, breath
and being with fuel so

Wherever you wish to go,
who am I to say don't?
but let me light a lamp
on the path you will walk

Hold My Hand

Flames of fire shall burn you not
Cold climes shall freeze you not
Deep waters shall drown you not
Ceaseless chasms shall bury you not

Hold my hand and have
a taste of eternity.

I am not a scholar nor a philosopher
Nor am I a heap of wisdom
I am just an emptiness
Have a brush with THIS
you shall Dissolve

Karma

When you mistake your
own Hand to be that of the
Divine. Either you shall
be bound by mirages of your
mind or you shall truly become
available to the beyond. Karmic
confusions can make you into an
apparition of delusions. Karmic
clarity can make you the
Master of your Destiny

Timeless Bond

Lifetimes of perseverance and toil
it took to build this timeless Bond.

Not just of love and longing
but to enmesh the innards of life.

A Bond beyond Age
A Bond beyond Bondage
A Bond that can beget
a lineage of love and light.

Thorns laid out upon the path
I walked in blissful unconcern.

The outpouring of my life
source of subtle rumble in your being.

Let not this taintless Bond
ever turn into a fruitless desert sand.

Touch my hand...

Touch my hand
Before my voice will falter

Sit with me
Until the shadows go

Become me
Before I am no more.

—— ..... ——

right Track

Even if you are on The right Track,
unless you are dynamic and move
quick, you could be Run Over.

Many Bridges we cross
create new possibilities that
take us across.
It is upon the backs of
those who build these
Bridges that we walk upon.

A Bridge is a device to cross over and touch
the other. If you could learn to build bridges
to people, communities, Nations, and to all
life, you shall become a Bridge that
liberates the world.

The Tree The Moon The Man

A prince wrapped in the folds
of regal pleasures and platitudes

Stung by the pain of ignorance
leaves all that a lesser man would cherish

The power of princehood, comfort of palace
warmth of a loving wife and joys of an infant son

The scourge of ignorance sears his mind
that he chooses to beg than be a Baron

The barrenness of not knowing
transforms into striving extraordinaire

The flower of knowing could not be denied
to the one who was a burning longing

The coolness of the full moon
An appropriate setting for the flowering

That cooled and quenched...
O' the blossoming of Knowing

Guru Pournami

In search of Truth
I did the sublime and the weird

The Blessed Guru arrived
Had my knowledge routed

With his staff touched the spot sacred
Left me with this Madness infected

This Madness without cure
But it is liberation for sure

When I saw even horrific disease
Can transmit with ease

I took the liberty
Of Maddening Humanity.

The Plunge

Plunge into the merciless
clarity that is me.
Clarity is neither an inoculation nor an armor
but the octane for the plunge

If one plunges willingly that is their heaven

What is a candle that was never burnt?
Un-burnt is unlit, unlit is unlived
To know the light of life
the pain of burning is all worth it

To burn willingly is to have no will of your own

With willingness, the shameful rape
becomes blissful love
With willingness, obliteration
becomes your ultimate liberation

Desire

Eternally Hungry flame
constantly licking at all
that it can touch, to digest
and combust the very Creation.
After endless pursuit to satiate
its hunger, still remains hungry.
This hunger to consume the
very Creation if it can, is also
the nature of Desire.
In desire you are not seeking
something to fill or fulfill
but to seek and taste the
very Creation and Creator.
May you burn as
a Cool Conscious fire that
shall not annihilate
but shall for sure
Light up the World.

Primal Call

Flowers of fragrance
The earthy soil
The body and soul
of this mortal coil
The rain drops fall
to mingle and spoil
Will you be there
For my Primal Call...

The Wall

A cricket's call could
be a heart-rending
love song. The growl
of the Tiger could be
of loneliness rather
than ferociousness. The
howl of the winds may
bring fortune of rain
and not a trail of
destruction. A serpent's
hiss not always venomous
Are you missing all calls
for Union and walling yourself
up against life.

Be or Busy

My Deepest song
has not been sung yet.
Still in wait for din to settle
and Silence to blossom.

When I sing that Song
Will you Be. Or Busy.

The Only Crime

If you do not burn in the raging fire that I am
you will never know life's sap as sham

If you do not see the life's seething sham
you will never know the grandeur of the other realm

If you do not know the taste of the other realm
forever you roll in this flesh and phlegm

To roll forever in this flesh and phlegm
not even knowing the caress of the divine hem

In the eternal scape the only crime.

When any being really yearns,
the Existence answers.
If the thirst within you is strong,
you can't go wrong.

A conch shell has risen from the ocean
Will you heed my call to awaken?
If for convenience you choose not to be shaken
Oceans will rise and you shall be forsaken.

My Master

Brooding, squinting, staring
I could not hit the mark
He walks in like a wanton monarch
With a crooked stick
And makes His Mark

My Master

Lost. Lost to life and death,
Both I did, but moved me not
A man who walks with a stick
Comes to me, the able-bodied one
Having seen birth and death
And all that life can bequeath
Still sitting dumbstruck,
Here comes the man with a stick
To have me struck
With his lightning stick.

My Master

I let the whole world go by
Of spiritual and material, of land and sky
I searched in the mother's womb and in the lover's bosom
But such a one I did not find
Till I crawled to him like a worm

My Master

What can the poor guru do?
All I have done is do and do
After seeing All that is there to see
He comes to Teach Me how to Be

My Master

The breath that passes out
Will not come back
The Guru who touched and left me
Left me not and need not come back.

————·····————

My Master's will
brought in a new skill
Obsessed with his will
did not bother if me it could kill

Pranam

My awareness knows yesterdays and tomorrows,
my love's domain is only today

Knowing the beginning and the end,
still have to play the game in the middle

The joy of love was coupled
with life-taking venom,
the wondrous grace of the Guru
with heart-breaking sadhana

The fire of enlightenment
with ridicule and failure
the blissfulness of the being,
the rapture of fulfillment, enjoined
with the pain of the body

Is this a joke
Is this Shiva's will
Is he compassion
Or cruel

O' Shambho! Let me tell one and all:
I do not want it any other way,
I do not want it any other way!

Of Truth

In pursuit of Truth
encountered many Perilous
situations and too many pernicious
people who are deeply invested
in Untruth.

In gratitude and Devotion for
My Master's will and the daunting
task of devising to spawn a
Divine form, had to bear
too many divisive and dastardly
sort invested in rapacity.

Now in efforts to inspire and infuse
Truth to the parched souls who
are losing the very basis of their
existential foundations, still
Headwinds of Ignorance and Insolence
The flight of Truth shall
Soar and Endure.

Lifetimes have passed by...

His wish and my will
Hardened into steely relentlessness
A resolve that broke through
the world's obstacles and traps
that were set and sustained by those
of ignorance and those in the know.

Knowing the fullness of fulfillment of purpose
Feels like a full Moon is stuck in my Heart
Oozing a cool glory of sheer existence.

Tenderness of too much life leaves me trembling
Thoughts and memories leave me in tears
So many of You, Your struggles, Your joy, Your love,
Your commitment and dedication. Above all Your
longing to know. Could die of this too much tenderness

But shall live for it.

Lifetimes have passed by...

Broken bowl

As my spirit soars
to Shiva's abode
Peak and pinnacle of
my mortal bowl
Shatter I did
the fictious soul
When spirit did
bounce to pinnacle pitch
break I did this empty bowl

To hold these pieces in position
I need you in utmost passion
Passion to burn, beyond reason
and blossom into my eternal season

When in you and me there is nothing uncommon
This bowl will hold, to be in wild abandon.

The Song (Geeta)

A hollow bamboo can
turn the passing Wind
into a Sweet Song.

One filled with his Own
Sap will be mute and dumb
When all of Creation laughs
and Sings.

If the hum of life's Sweet Song
has to be heard, empty. Empty
yourself of yourself.

The Sweetness, the Melody, and the Fragrance
of the Divine Song shall be You.
When you let yourself be absorbed
into the Master's Will.

My Lap

My lap holds no Mysteries
Just an empty space, offers
room for an endless pursuit
A pursuit that is an end in
itself. My lap offers stillness
on the inside and exuberance of the
outer. Exuberance of the within
will lead to lunacy and
stillness of the outer is Death.

Lay upon my lap,
Know the unmoving exuberance of
the Borderline Being
who is here very much and
yet Not. Lay upon my lap
to Be and Not to Be.

Of flames

As flames lick up in lustful
hunger to quench their
seemingly endless thirst to burn
all into constance of Ash.

Flames that can burn the world
down, not just a home.
Tamed by the simple
arrangement of a fireplace.
Simple rearrangement of
your thought, emotion and
Body you shall harness the
fire of life to the constance
of Compassion, love and Bliss

Unmaking

Those who feed upon the written word
Claim to know the limits of the boundless beyond

In the realm of the beyond
Clueless is the scholarly dud

The gloriousness of the written word
Is but the excreta of the deluded mind

If in you a raging longing I have made
Don't you quench it with the delusions of the mind

Allow yourself to be unmade
Into the vastness of the beyond you will be made

ETERNAL SOUND

No one is mine
Nor am I of anyone
I am just an empty Shell
I resonate like a conch
That is dry and dead but
captures the Sacred Sound.
Only in being bereft of all
that one values as Self
does this genderless life
echo the Eternal Sound

Absence

If you are enamored with my presence
O you should taste my absence

If my presence has made some sense
In my absence you would know the true essence

In my presence if you did find some romance
My absence would bring you to utter obeisance

In my presence if you have been swept by my grace
My absence will take you beyond grace and disgrace

If my presence has been an intoxicating wine
My absence will drown you in Divine

MYSTICAL

Realm of the Mystic

Even a blade of grass is pointing towards you
A pine tree of course is reaching out for you
Every pulsating cell of protoplasmic shell
Has to ceaselessly tread your mindless will
My longing and thrashing was a veritable hell
This merging has become blissful and still

Now I can say your Will is my Will
And when I Will, you Will.

Romancing the Source

Silence not of Death
but of roaring life

Silence not of suppression
but of profound submission

Submission not to the senses
or the senselessness of the society

Submission to the source
that is within and without

Consummating with the
Silence of the Source

Silence

The Silence of the Sages is
not in pursuit of endless mirages.
To decipher the difference of mirages
and moksh from the world of mirages
One longing to cross the sands of time
and space to foray into terrains unknown
will have much to seek and nothing to speak.
In traversing the travesty of Time and Space
Too much magic to imbibe and digest.
The glory of the grand creation on a closer look
can only leave you Speechless.

So is Silence a Choice...

SHADOWLESS

Two lives can become one
The hope of every lover.
The longing to be enjoined
with another life is a longing
for completeness of life's experience.

The Beauty is not togetherness
but of near perfect alignment
Like the shadow and its source
being alike in moments
of rare perfection. But alas
life is of the moving sort.
As the light source moves the
shadows will not align with
the source. They wax and wane
with every passing moment.

The opacity of your Being brings
shadows of umpteen kind.
In knowing the transparence
of One's Being, shall you know the
shadowless existence of perfect Alignment

Culmination

My Poetry is not by intent
but a natural consequence of
the way I am. I am like
a dry stick of logic with
an effusion of flowering. When
a lush green plant bears flowers
it could be lost in its own exuberance.
But when a dry stick spouts
an outpouring of blossom, it
just cannot be missed.

So is creation, the vast barren
scape of emptiness bears the
multitude of life, not by intent
but a natural expression of
meticulous conservation that bursts
forth into unimaginable beauty
and scintillating energy. All from
the seemingly lifeless space – scape.

I am not cultivated with
education, etiquette or civilization
I am just a natural Culmination

Salt Doll

In search of truth
did I go back and forth

Wandered through Mountains
bathed in rivers sacred, with the pious

Whichever way the blind pointed
with hope and zest me travelled

Every which way I smelled the scent
but round and round is all I went

Wasted lives to know the one who is not
but the feverish pitch of seeking would cease not

What does it take to fathom the ocean
even fish or whale is clueless of the ocean

It is only the salt that can be ocean
a Salt Doll I became, just a plunge made me the ocean.

When I Lost My Sense

Then I was a man
I only went up the Hill
As I had time to kill
But kill I did all that was
Me and Mine

With Me and Mine gone
Lost all my will and skill
Here I am, an empty vessel
Enslaved to the Divine Will
and infinite skill

...the Scent

I sought no other
than the all Seeing One
I sniffed up anything or
anyone who had a bit of
that scent

———·····———

The comfort of a pleasant
valley shall not hold me
down from the harsh Mountains.
Propelled by that One Mountain Dweller,
You see.

———•••••———

Men became Monks
Not just to meditate
But to moult out of manliness
To moult from mundane to mystic

———•••••———

Sanyas

This stance of nakedness,
An effort to strip the soul
Armed with nakedness and a bowl
The glorious one made it to the goal.

My loss

When I lost all that was me
When I lost all that I had
The very basis of my self
All thought I had found
and they gather around
to relish in my loss
To listen to my emptiness
bereft of a soul or self.
Just an echo...

Beyond as Beloved

To be a human Being
Is to become a bridge
To make far near
And the Beyond your Beloved

Bliss

In faraway lands am I
but as near to you as ever

I've infused my life energies in you
and you are no more yourself but me

You are among the privileged few
who seek the creator

My blissfulness is my only blessing
You should know the bliss that is me

Restless

Ever since You infused into my Being
My eyes have not known rest
Eyes open I see only you in all
Eyes closed I neither know
thought nor contemplation or Dream
Just your wild Dance unnuanced
Or the death defying stillness
My eyes know no rest nor respite
With the all seeing One infused in Me.

This blessed restlessness
This relentless assault upon My Being
Please do not stop, Do not stop.

———•••••———

To become able to see
what most fail to see
is empowerment. Only
what you perceive is real
rest is imagination.

———•••••———

Creation the only doorway to the Creator.
Irreverence to the Creation will ensure
doors to the Divine shut.

Idea of Creation

All our ideas are nothing
as we ourselves are the
Idea of Creation.

———·····———

Creation

The swirling mist in the
valley, causes haze in me
like the Hashed-out mind
of a yogi. Haze not of hallucination
But like the haze of the Beginnings

Substance Abuse

To be sober is dreary
But inebriation takes you
away from all that is reality
How to dwell in the empty
room of dry lifeless logic.
Logic through the day and
inebriation at the end of the day
logic through the week and
inebriation for the weekend
logic at work and inebriation
for the vacation. Say the compromisers

Come! I have a substance
that leaves you in throes of ecstasy
And peak of alertness at once.
No need for secrecy, no one
will find us in our within.

Let us abuse the substance
without dimension but within
let us get super sober and stoned

Unknowing

Many layers of the Hills
Green in shades too many
The tantalizing Mist working
its Magic to veil and unveil
many visions that could engage
a Keen mind into visions and
delusions unknown. Off these
Misty slopes have risen the
fabulous and the fearful.
Many manifestations of the
Mind Space. One who attempts
to capture will conjure false
Visions of hidden ghosts
not of these mountains but of Mind.
One who unfolds the
Mind Space to these Misty mountains
shall clear all mist of the Mind
to have crystal clear space
beyond knowing and Unknowing.

Of Waiting

When it comes to the
Divine, there is no difference
between the Man and the Beast
It is only in waiting that you
shall know the Eternal

———·····———

Not of will but willingness
Shall make the stones melt. Turn walls into grand
Doorways. Gods emerged from stones you see.

———•••••———

Tree that bears fruit
gives not of itself
but only sweetens the bounty
of the all giving earth.
The fruit seller
brings it to your doorstep.
The ultimate fruit
an offering not a transaction.

———•••••———

Have you heard of an
Ocean that went up the
Mountain and turned sweet
Manasarovar and Me too.

———•••••———

This breath that binds you to body
Can a means to unbind be
A passage to heaven will unfold
If your breath you let me steal.

The Source

As fragrance that lies in Jasmine
waiting for the blossoming
As a vibrant butterfly waits within
the lifeless cocoon
As the brilliance of the sun
waits behind the shadowy night

The Divine awaits beneath the veil
of ignorance, a product of
illusory boundaries drawn by
the insecure creature, to lift.

The effulgence of the Divine obscured
by the fog of mental malice.
A seemingly endless thought
and emotion weaving webs
of Maya. In efforts to find
Comfort sacrificing the very Cosmic
In the blossoming of this
Being lies the Source.

The Bond

But then I belonged to earth
Simple, Earthy, Deep
The creatures of the earth loved me so deep
The humans were out behind a step
And found me too steep

With that of camphor and moonlight meet
Love's compulsions in passion met

Inebriated by the hypocrisy of
Their sacred sect
Plotted to murder love's breast
'n' sweetness of the venom did put me to rest

Another man's seed did bloom in your womb
But you in your steadfastness did not let it exit

But the infant life did force
Its right to exit
And put the restless you
Into stone like rest

Since the spirits
Raged in mutual pursuit

The earth became the sky
But the moonlight did wax and wane

Moonlight could bond and blend
The still sky to the earthy earth

Or the lack of it could put the
Earth back to earth
And let the spirit to eternal rest

Touch the Divine

Even the Umbilical Cord
has to be broken for life
to thrive. From then on
the nature of Human Life
makes many a bond and breaks
quite a few. Like the Seed
that sprouts has to break its
bond with the shell that
sheltered it, to make a
larger bond with the
Earth and the Sky.
Bonds of love, companionship,
nourishment and blood
all shall be broken for
one who longs to grow
and touch the Divine.

———•••••———

You may either Hide
or you may Seek
The domain of the Divine
is open to all who Seek

———•••••———

To reach out beyond your present
levels of perception is the only
way to touch the Divine.

And to touch the Divine is to
know the Bliss of your existence.

———•••••———

The taste of life
can leave you heady
But if you imbibe enough
the source will clear your head

NagPanchami

If it was not for the Serpent
Adiyogi would be without a
moving ornament. The first
dumb couple would be twiddling
their thumbs, denied even
of their basic physical purpose.
I would not have espied
the ways of the Creation and Creator
Nor would I know when to
shift gears for accelerated and
smooth function of Shiva's Will.

If it was not for the Serpent...

Ye Devi

Pregnant with a Divine form
As a man I break all norm

As a bee knows how to craft its hive
Seemingly aimless, does purposefully strive

Sting that can punch poisoned pain
Crafts sweetness that one's dearest can only fain

This dark and fiery divine wench
You have no need that she cannot quench

Give yourself to the Three-Eyed One
In the world of maya you have won

To the yet to be

The gentle coolness of the morn
Heralding the day that is to be born

Like the voiceless struggles of the unborn
The light struggles not to be too soon

Having explored the mysteries beyond horizon
Have arrived at this blessed twilight zone

As a whimsical wench holds my life thread that is worn
Now will deny to many the mysteries of the new morn

As the frog croaks like a fog horn
I sit still in the knowing, I will never be born

...I Sleep

In the lap of my Creator, I lie.
When in sleep, I am His.
In wakefulness with all my striving I am bound too.
Bound in enslavement to all the ignorance and insanity,
of the wretchedness of the world,
But in sleep I am His.

Innocent and pure as I should always be.
Please do not wake me up,
I long to awaken in my sleep.
If only you could be awake and asleep at once,
You would be in the lap of the Divine for always.

Temple

Designing for the Divine
Is only imitation in converse
of the Designs of the Divine.

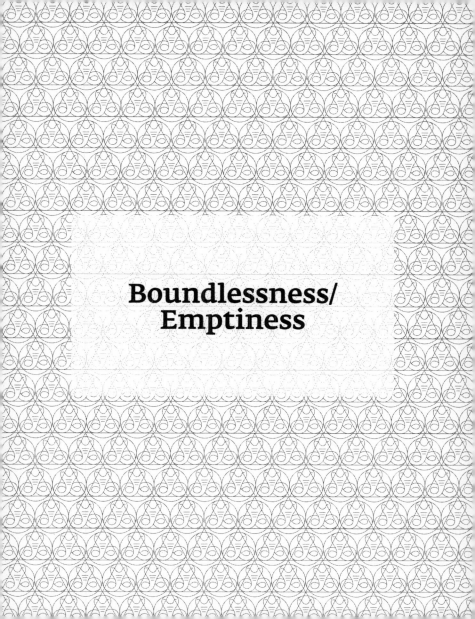

Boundlessness/
Emptiness

Boundless

Home is the sailor, home from the seas
Home is the farmer, home from the fields
Home is the hunter, home from the hills

In the twilight wonder
I look up in the sky for a home
Even the birds are homing

Home, home – home for what
Is it of brick and mud for security and shelter
Or is it of love, companionship and comfort

Homes of shelter and security
or love and comfort
No homes for me

Shambho, my only home
Homeless he is and homeless am I,
Boundless

Limitless

The limitless energy
dances in many limited ways

The limited so complete
that it thinks it is its own

The limited and the limitless:
where is the line unless you draw one

The illusion of the limited:
the source of longing and pain

A taste of the unlimited leaves you
drenched in Bliss Divine

Makes the pleasure and pain of life
sweeter by the zillion

Empty

How shall I tell you
my predicament!

Would thinking minds
ever know the brilliance in me
that would put the poor sun to shame

And it is not me

Would curious minds
ever know the ecstasy
that this grave visage masks

And it is not me

Would objective minds
ever know that these stern eyes could exude
love that could turn stones into beating hearts

And it is not me

Oh, how shall I tell you
my predicament!

I am empty but full

Full

The wind blows not so gentle
The leaves rustle ever so mournful
My heart stirs in unseason joyful
Love mocks ever so scornful
Time flows just mindful
This empty me, full full

No Pain or Gain

I live a life where there is
No pain or gain
Even the butterfly or the bird
Cannot imagine to soar
As I do upon wind and rain
Or just the emptiness of the sky

As I am what I breathe
touch and cannot touch
I courted the Boundless
Ended up with the blessed Emptiness
I am for all and all is for me
I have no pain or gain

Boundless Bubble

There are days that are meaningful
For all that i do and much others do.
There are days that are meaningless
but fabulous devoid of puny acts
of meaning and usefulness.

But there are days that are just Empty.
Meaningless, useless, bereft of beauty.
Just grateful that there is an
Existence beyond me and within.
Boundless Bubbled up in Me.

NIRGUN

As there is nothing that
I truly call as mine,
neither this Body nor Anybody,
neither this World nor the Other
Neither Friends nor Foes belong.
No fear of Losing, no anticipation of Gain.
Here i am a Transparence without Substance.
A Presence without Persona.
A Being without Self.

Hence activity has become Stillness
The Din of the world my Silence
The very Cosmos my Being.

Satori

The cosmic spectacle
This spectacular splash
is but a spot in the space
of my borderless Being

Is this the story of the
Fly upon an Elephant?

Nay it is the Satori
of borderless Magic
Where shapes and sizes
are but a delusion

Empty Page

When thoughts that are
too profound for words
form in one's mind
Heart swells, lifts tides high
The veil of time cracks and
reveals the roots of past
and what pretends as future

A man who lives through this
is no more just a man
The world will label him a sage
But in truth he is a fathomless empty page

———•••••———

Only in crossing the limitation of physical
One will know the Blissfulness of spirit

———•••••———

Open a door and there is an
entire new world of possibilities and perceptions

∞ 4/16

The longing for the Infinite
From infancy gave me eyes that
looked beyond what lay before me.
This far-away look was not for
the far or the near
But for not being finite
As all that is finite has a
bond that I could recognize
but could not reconcile.

The Glory and Ecstasy of the
Infinite showered itself
in abundance to make me
human in ways that most
humans have never explored
In ways that obliterate the
line between human and divine.

But the finite has its fun
and fanfare. The world is finite
So is the body and so is the mind
and so is all creation.

Creation and all forces of creation
just a complex number game
All of it having their play
within the boundaries of the Zero.

Infinite 'o' (zero) has bred all
this numerical magic.
Though my domain is of the Infinite
I do well with the number game too.

Nothing

As all aspired to conquer
the finite that ever multiplies
The seemingly foolish Me let
the infinite conquer me.

I remain innocent to the
Powers and Pleasures of a king
or conqueror. But revel in
the Ecstasy of Abandon.
Unmindful that I have been
invaded by the Infinite.
A force that destroys your
person and all the attendant
concerns, to render you
to be Blameless, Sinless, Homeless.
Not just less than someone
but a boundless – Nothing

———•••••———

An agile life gathers
Nothing. The Nothing is worth
more than all the somethings

———•••••———

Keep your innards still
To know the boundless will
Then all you capture
Will only be rapture

The Boundless has been bound

The Boundless has been bound
The beauty of the limited
Obscures the Unlimited
The puny Man overshadows the Divine
The many foldedness of the echo
Shall not obliterate the Eternal

Shameless

Of virtue and shame
All arguments a game

The shamelessness of a slut
The lifeless copulation of glorified spouse
Of the shameless and the lifeless
Which a greater crime?

The strength of shoulder, of donkey in prime
Would make a well bred horse stand in shame
The left over plateful would make the beggar well
And leave the king in raging hell

The boundless being that I am
Know neither virtue nor shame

O virtuous of the world
Till you know the boundlessness of who I am
Shame, shame, it's all a crime

The fraudulent few...

Among the fraudulent few
resides many a great sage
In rampant barrage of
rudimentary logic of the materialist.
Seers and Sages suffer the
ignominy of the worst sort.
Yogis and Mystics will face
ridicule and possible persecution.
As commercial forces reign
Supreme reducing human mind
to a marketplace of give and take.
Subtle fragrance of life
may yield to the crude concubine
of commerce and corruption.
Time for humanity not to wait
but to wake up and raise the
Subtle force of consciousness.
From the mad stupor of consumption
to the fulfilment of Conscious living.
From the limitation of cheap wine
To the wild abandon of Divine.
From the fraudulence of the few
To the rapture of the Boundless.

Dark Bounty

A tiny flame flickers
fragile in the nightly
gathering of impregnable
Darkness Dark

Seemingly waging a lonely
battle against this
boundless bounty

That is the basis of
all that is and not

Empty Face

The blindness of the Bat
got covered by the unheard
sound. Do you have
something to cover your
ignorance? Are you just
a farce of a scripture or
a teaching? Are you the
fraudulent One who nurtures
a secret will or fanciful
whim? Or are you kneaded
by the Masters Will? Do you
cohabit with Masters Grace?

Are you an empty Face
An expression of His Grace

Living Mind

The Mind that makes life
Pulsing mass of No-Thing
Boundless and no less
Not more or less
Just borderless
Infinite, Endless
Words and Words
That State Nothing
Defining the Definitionless
That which Is, Only Is.
Isn't that which is Not
Shiva

Darkness and Light

Dark Light

In the darkest crevices
of one's being lies light

Light that shines only for the ones
that sink into the very depths of darkness

Light, the one light that
cannot be dispersed into seven

The seven that scaffolds the
fragile life of elements five

Me found light to become
as dark as darkness can be

That turned me into light for those
that grope in darkness for light

The Dark One

When I first heard the sounds of
Darkness and silence meeting within me

The little mind argues for light
The virtue, the power, the beauty

Light a brief happening could hold me not
All encompassing darkness drew me in

Darkness the infinite eternity
Dwarfs the happened, the happening and yet to happen

Choosing the eternal
Darkness I became

The dark one that I am
The divine and the devil are but a small part

The divine I dispense with ease
If you meet the devil you better cease

Isha Fest

This world of light and darkness
Creating illusions of changing perspectives
Did hold me dear and far
Light in day's delight stark
Darkness of night's pleasures deep and dark
Then this descent of neither darkness nor of light
Leaving me in throes of neither life nor death
Taking away all perspectives of darkness and light
Leaving me in a state that is formless, nameless, senseless,
lifeless, deathless and of course boundless
My intelligence and my life is a struggle to
channelize into sensible proportions
This me of unbridled and wild abandon

———•••••———

From the darkness of the womb
to the deceptive light of the world
but the journey is not complete
until you see in the darkness of the cosmic womb.

———•••••———

When you get the angles Right
within and without there shall be Light

Firefly

In the moonless night
the firefly emboldens itself to flight

The brooding darkness mocks
the spirited flight of fly delight

The limitless darkness could
swallow this miniscule attempt of light

The skeptics' cantankerous laughter
swept the inner spaces within me to ask:
Can a firefly light the world?

Yes, firefly am I

If life's summers have warmed you,
your inner spaces have charmed you,
I could set you afire, and the world too

light for the Blind

Fire of my Mind
Fire of my Heart
Fire of my Body
Immense fire of my Being
I Condensed into cool fire

The coolness of my fire
makes my fire unconditional
Doesn't feed upon life giving oxygen
Underwater or in ice or in cold space
My fire flourishes to be light

Light that is beyond senses
light that is eternal

light that even the blind can know.

light up your Blindness
with my cool fire

Inner Way

As the sun slips off our horizon
To warm and nourish other time zones
As dear darkness descends in quietness
Pushing our part of the world into dark coolness
Many a man and woman wanting a rest from toil
Industrious and boisterous,
may choose to burn the night's oil

The forest of the insects, birds and beasts come to a boil
They start their conversations in high decibel
Saying things that you would say the following day
That is all you can say, unless you know the inner way

From darkness to light
a cracker of a journey

Enlight

As darkness descends upon this gentle earth
one half of life prepares to rest upon her breast
another half begin their nightly quest

Me, a creature of neither day nor night,
stares into this awesome darkness
that is the source of light

This womblike darkness of night delight
made light by songs of the creatures of the night
their incessant rancor for food or mate
makes me see light beyond day and night

I cannot see darkness or light
ever since this darkness bright

LOVE and DEVOTION

...the fall

Looking out at the Valley
seems like the sky is attempting
to fit into the earth or the
cloud that we see as fluff in
the sky has fallen into the Valley.

As all things that fly has to
land or fall. The same fate
for a stone or star that they
need to fall. Yes we must fall.
Now to make falling a beautiful
phenomenon fall in love, devotion
or in surrender as to
fall is free

Heart Wrung

These pinks and blues
And the quaint lavender lies

A desperate cover for
The winter's bareness true

My being in a sprightly spring
But my heart in winter's wring
Only you have the balm
To put my heart to sprightly spring
And free from winter's wring

Call it what you want

The winds of love blowing
Through me, through every pore
There is mischief in my heart
That longs to tease you,
Every cell of you

I look for you behind
Every leaf, flower and
In vain upturn every pebble in the field

There is joy in just waiting for you
Am I condemned to know
Only the tearful joy of waiting?
Is this wretch destined forever to keep
A part of himself in another's nest?

Koel does keep its own
In another's nest
Only to recover at the
First sign of flighty wing
To show its true nature and sing

The song in my heart
Will it forever be stifled?

Or will it before my
Time be buried?

To be a vain love that
Will be just remembered?

The Divide

Is it the lines
drawn by the unseen
hand

Is it the lines
traversed by the planets
and stars

Is it the lines
drawn by the social norms
and taboo

Is it the lines
etched upon one's hands
or feet

Is it the lines
of one's prejudice
and pride

Lost in this needless
intrigue, one lets life
go by

Never shall most humans
explore the borderless
nature of one's being

Lines have no meaning
for a being lost in love

Rainbow

Are you black, brown, white or red
or are you someone with a working head?

In every little thing variety you seek,
skin colors you reject: look at your cheek

The god in heaven, you proclaim and exhort,
but his creation you fight and reject

Have you not soaked this planet
with our own blood and senseless hate?

O man will you stand up and tread
the path of loving heart and working head

Love Fatal

Above the clouds we float
In a metal can, most so
oblivious to the fragile nature
of this aluminum can, with
engines and seats to sit in
comfort or discomfort. A few
miles above mother earth
who has a relentless love to
embrace and include all
into her bosom. This ceaseless
love is overwhelming but
Fatal.

My Secret

Let me tell you my Secret
I have not one but two hearts
One that always bleeds
Another that rejoices in all
One that bleeds for the Worm
Another rejoices for the Bird
Bleed I do for the Vanquished
Rejoice I will for the Victor
Death of a worm, insect, bird
animal or man and of course
of the plant and tree, I bleed
I rejoice all that is life
Here and After.

Cake in a glass case

"Someone loves you!"
"love is in the air!"
"god is love!"

Unless love sprouts
in your Heart
Are all like Cake
in a glass case
can make your
mouth water
But shall never nourish you.

Love

A scratch of the pen
A flick of the tongue
A look of the eye
A touch of the hand
These are all the ways.

My love

Will you shear
My body
Will you skim
my mind
Or will you
pierce my heart
I shall become
your toy or tool
or love.

Woman

These creatures of the moon
in such delicious swoon
the sun in me not the only boon
to these creatures of the moon

Daily death, a must for the sun,
to be kept and nourished
In the pregnancy of the moon
It is her gracious reflection
that sees him through the night

Sun, the source of all known creation,
is but born in the coolness of the moon
The Creator placed such trust
in this unreasonable madness of the moon
Bestowed the womb to bear
and the feeding breast

May she flower and bloom too soon:
only then can there be worthwhile harvest
When the world knows the nourishment
of this womb,
in celebration will exist
these creatures of the moon.

Samskriti

For an Individual to blossom
Into eternal straits of Freedom
A culture of ceaseless love and Devotion
Unconcerned with material outcome.

The Divine yields not
to the ritual of worship
But only to heartfull courtship.

Ocean of devotion

Lustful looks of one who lacks love.
Loving touch of a heart that is soaked in the infinite will,
The tenderness of heartless devotion,
Vast beyond the measure of an ocean.
Barrenness of one, who knows not the grace of love and
devotion,
All this and more are the ways of the creature called human.
Choose my beloved to be an ocean of devotion.

Love

Love for you, is it
a fancy or a feeling?
or just a lustful longing?
In me it is not just a fancy feeling
But a glorious burning
that I aspire will consume me
To bring to that which is
Immortal and Immaculate.

Fortune it is for the mortal vermin
to burn in the glory of this immortal fire

Oh, how many a mortal vermin
did murder this marvel
for mundane concerns.

Do fan the glorious fire
to melt and merge.

Those who know the fortune of merging
Shall no more mortal be.

Tapas

The incessant chant
of a God that will not come

There is no instance of
him coming to anyone that called

How can he come when
he is not there, but
here and everywhere

What sort of call is yours
I've heard insects call,
birds call, cats call, apes call
What is needed is not your call
but you to fall

He no creature to respond to calls
You will know his repose
only when you let your
walls fall and dissolve

Linga Bhairavi

Seek her in Devotion
She is an ocean of Compassion

Seek her in Desperation
She is a steadfast Companion

Seek her in true Passion
You will be loved to Distraction

Just seek her in your Confusion
She will lead you to Fruition

Jai Bhairavi Devi

Vijji

She knew Love
and nothing more

She was Love
and nothing more

The lord needs Love
and nothing more

She wooed him with Her Love
and She is no more

LOVE

Love as many think
is not just an emotion
But a rail that guides
Our thought and emotion
from the barrenness of
exclusion to the harvest
of inclusive existence.
Love is not just a bond
But a balloon that buoys
you to the borders of Boundlessness.

Inner Delight

The stark barrenness of the desert
stood as mute reflection of my heart

The thirst of the parched tongue
was puny to my heart's longing
The waterless dry death of the desert
would be relief to my love's longing

This merciless longing
not seeking any belonging

The toils of the endless day
the lonesomeness of the longer night
amalgamated into brightness bright
soaking me in an inner delight

The merciless longing and lack of belonging
led me on into the wonderment of dissolving

Knowing

Shall I call this
A longing or love
Or just my way
Of seeing and being.

Lovin'

Selfless action roots you
in love unbounded,
unbounded love is the
stepping stone for limitless joy

When you are joy there is meditation
meditativeness, the only freedom

No special occasion just for love

to my Father

You never figured
the guile of this world.
but still served with
absolute devotion to all
you could.

You were always stumped
by the many things that
your children became
but did not fail to support
or celebrate their success

As a Husband, our Beloved Mother
said there could be no better.

Your innocuous Presence has been
Impressive

———·····———

A man is a true Man only in
learning to serve with joy.

———·····———

How can you love one and hate the other
when the same divine exists in all beings.

Inner Ice...

If you melt the inner Ice
with your love for all life,
life is full of spice.

———•••••———

If there is no awareness
let there be at least tenderness

Tenderness

Tears of too much tenderness
Well up in my eyes
My bosom swells
Not with love nor compassion
But with tenderness
That links my being with all.

Too tender even to touch
Leave alone embrace

I need to coat myself
With a coat of bravado
Even to touch the breath of another
As to touch would be
To terminate my existence.
An embrace would erase
All that is perceived as me.

Tears of too much tenderness
Well up and my bosom swells.

Tenderness

The irony of life
that I should now
be doing everything to bind myself

To demarcate boundaries
that no one should cross,
doing my best to be self-centered

All these antics just to keep
this crumbling cage intact
'With the work done, why linger on?
Depart gracefully', says my mind

But what to do with lovers
who have lost themselves in the
process of loving?

Too many lovers, the very remembrance
bring tears of too much tenderness
So I'll act brash and go on

Too Much Tenderness

One very Dear to me
is gone, leaving a gentle
fragrance of love and grace
But a heavy burden of Absence

The vacuum of Absence
is ever willing to fill up
Fill it with Grief of the deprived
Or with the gentle presence
of Grace and Gratitude for a
life that enjoined you with
love and beauty when in Presence

May you enjoy the Bounty
of too much Tenderness in Absence.

Wayward

The way of the wayward
Breaks all social structures
Moral and ethical lies shattered
Love is the only quotient
Love not of unbridled mating
But to enjoin in the immensity
Of the Ultimate Meeting

Beyond Love

This universe is but a minuscule
In the vastness of my inner spaces

My love for you is but a ploy
To retain this little toy (body)

I know neither love nor longing
As all that is, is me

You an unlimited possibility
Have settled to be a limited diversity

Your exclusiveness, you enshrined
But my inclusiveness cannot be chained

When it is just me, me and me alone
Why this you and me?

Tread Gently

Tread gently O' Ishas!
I've let you seep into
The minute crevices of my body
Where life entrenched itself

Encompassing you all into this
Pulsating mass of flesh
I've become eternally pregnant

This rapture, this pain, this fullness
I am unable to bear, but love and longing
Will never let you part

This flesh, blood, breath and being
Are soaked with you

Your every thought, word and deed
Penetrates the life preserving crevices of the body

Tread in love, compassion and awareness
For all that you tread is only me

Ocean

An ocean refuses no river
In the ocean of my love
There is space for you,
for him, for her, for this and that
If you have touched the ocean
No point thinking of rivulets
and streams that brought you
In only becoming the salt of its salt
Can one know the ocean.

My Heart My Arms

If I had kept my
Heart to myself I could
love you. If I kept my arms
to myself, I would have held you.
But mashed my heart and spread
it across the globe. My arms are
in tight embrace of the Planet.
If you have to escape my Heart
or my Arms, you have to be someplace
else. Someplace beyond this
Universe and beyond my imagination.
For One who is beyond why
would you need love

My Magic, My Miracle

The fluctuations of the mental
firmament
Set forth chemical throes
of pleasure and torment
Sensations bitter and sweet
make you fret and pant.
These cycles of pleasure or torment
are rave and rant of enslavement
Letting you go beyond this cycle
Is my only Magic and Miracle.

Fabric of Light

In my efforts to drape
the world in Fabric of Light
This physical fabric
has seen weakening and
wear. Needs to strengthen
before the tear, with
strands of youthfulness
dyed in Devotion
and Dare. Strands of
love beyond lust. Devotion
beyond doubt. Involvement
beyond individuality.
Only with these strands
can you weave a Fabric
of Light. Yes I want
the world to be clothed
in light. As the naked
will choose to remain
in the Dark.

Sugarcane

Far has your heart gone
To know the sweetness of loves hurt

The hardy cane somehow
Did manage the sweetness of sugar

But this hardness will yield its
Sweetness only in brutal crush

Though I have no stomach
To brutalize my beloved you

If your hard shell will not let your
Sweetness ooze
I will have no qualms to set you to
The noose
To make you sweet
As sweetness ever was

TOIL

PUFFS

Every Human Being a Buffoon
To believe in the individual
Nature of one's own Being
Puffs of cloud hang out
each as if they are of their own.
A gentle breeze will merge
them to terminate their individuality.

A small change in atmosphere shall
bring it down pouring to meet and mingle
with Mother Earth who anyways
is the source of these sky soaring puffs.

O' Buffoon may you not puff up
in pride only to come pouring down.

Peril of Pride

Of anger, hate, greed and Pride
which is a greater folly
Anger for sure will make
you burn and cause distress
or death to the other. Hate
surrogate of anger, more
overt and consuming but
a child of anger. Greed
seems to have nothing to do
with the above two but breeds
anger and hate towards all
that thwart the insatiable
fire of greed. As there is not
anything that can fulfill the
gastronomy of greed.
Pride though looks pretty
and makes one perky
takes the pride of place
in destroying all possibilities
of human kind. As it is
the pride that sets one
upon a perch that deceives

Reality. A perch that
makes unreal real and the
Truth into Untruth
Anger, hate and greed
need the theater of Pride
to play. Pride is a crown
of thorns that makes
one perceive even pain as
pleasure. Pride is the
Maya, the delusion of life.
Refinement of ignorance
Is not Enlightenment.

Of Bonds and Bondage

Beautiful bonds of love
turn into ugly bondage
Not 'cause of someone turned
ugly or treacherous or plain evil.
When you tried to bend
the beautiful bond to tilt
in your favor. When you
started thinking what is my
take away – you took away
the Beauty and turned
a tango into a transaction.
Transactions could have brought
Profits but reaped poison
within, turning the beautiful
Bond into Bondage

Walls of self-protection are also walls of
self-imprisonment. What to say of bombs
and bunkers, war never gets over
in this me versus you.

Whether Fireballs fly
in offense or defense
their source is fear or hate.
The cool fire of consciousness
Its time has come.

Woman

How much prejudice
towards the very womb
that bears us.

Though there are claims
of men being born without
a father, there is no
instance of a birth without
a Mother. No society can
Exist or Flourish without
Empowering the Feminine

An ode to the humiliated

Oh Humiliated ones
I know your pain
The faceless pain of
Unending depth
If it turns into anger
In torrents it would run
But the simple humiliation
Of being able but by volition unable
When strings of life
Tie your hands
It becomes not death
But deeper death

JUSTICE

What is Just need not be Humane
As Judges and Jury not only
of the legal systems but those
who proliferate homes, streets
organizations and media houses.
They are all over, doing
Marsupial justice quick and irrevocable.
Before one can defend, they have
moved on to the next case.
You case number ooo have no right
to bask in the glorious morning
Sun. As you have been judged
World moves on.
Everyday a Judgement Day.

Jesus

Parentage bereft of love and pleasure
Denied the pleasure of walking
terra firma. Evil and ignorant
ones nail him to woodwork
perhaps reward for being a
carpenter. In two thousand
years all who claim to love him
refuse to bring him down
from the cross. When the
source within has risen
this is what you do.

Nail the living
worship the dead

———•••••———

If you do not know how
to walk upon water, best you
learn to Swim. If did walk
upon water, where would you swim....

———•••••———

If carpets could fly
The rules of nature you wouldn't comply

Kashmiri, Tibetan, Persian or Turkish
Or plain gibberish. Only if you comply – you fly.

Down The Heaven

Of many Crimes that
humans can perpetrate upon
each other, the worst of all
Crimes is Heaven.

. For those who have not
eaten well there is great food
up there. For those who
like their drink there are
rivers of wine up there if only
they abstain here.

For those who are deprived
of their lustful longings here
there are virgins in golfy
proportions up there.

When will men live
a fulfilling life Here...

To destroy Heavens and make
this planet a Paradise is Mission One
let us make it Happen.

Make up your Mind

A Mountain is god
A River is god
A Tree is god
Make up your mind
are you...Or
do you have to get
to heaven first.

Beheading

Fighting for gods and scriptures
of another place and time.
Their relevance you may Question
if only you do not value your
own life. Heads have been rolling for a
long time for sensitivities that
are not for Life.

In not making anything of value of Oneself
has such an advantage of being welcomed
in another place that is haloed
and divine that is worth killing for.

Those who had nothing of much
value in their Heads, always
believed separating Head
from Body is a solution.

1976

All the things that bother me
were not about myself or someone
I knew. Worried about the
Revolution in Korea, Skull mountain
of Cambodia, Yellow gas in Vietnam
Mao's message in China, Castro's
tears in Cuba, Segregation and beatings
in America, Caste Castigation in
the badlands of India. Corruptions
of Governments, Religion and pillars
of Society. Discriminatory inhumanity
among verity of Humans who could
suspend their Humanity to
their convenience with relative
Blindness and mute by choice.
I wondered will I just worry myself
to death or find a way to transform
...and hence turned inward

Human longing to find meaning
Has led them into past legends preening
Knowing is not in looking forward or backward
Upward or downward. But only inward.

Adiyogi

An Inspiration beyond
divisiveness. An Icon
for Human liberation.
From Religion to Responsibility.

Your Choice

Human thought and emotions
fed by images and impressions of Senses,
ancestry and Cultural Conundrum.
Senses giving half images of all
that they capture in their web.
Seemingly unrelated images and
ancestral voices of lives forgotten
Of lives unmentioned in the written
word of that day or this.

Many lives of times forgotten
Can twitch and turn or find rhythm
and dance. Ancestry plays not just
through genetic seed but much more
through the Cultural Conundrum

Thoughts are intermingled, emotions
entwined and lives fused.
Does this make you One big mess
Or an exotic Magic
is but
Your choice

Regality

That which comes out of deceit, treachery
and spilling of blood — is this regality or vulgarity?
All that is left is an arrangement of stones
If you must move stones, let there be love
and devotion. This pathetic toil for glory
would become an abode of the divine.

Final Destiny

Will there be a world
without Nations. Will there
be a world without borders
Will there be a nation without
divisions. Will there be people
without conflicts. Will there
be a day when we do not
have to kill each other to possess
land, that anyway is our
final Destiny

Of Nations

National borders, not to cut
the world into useless scraps
of geography and endless prejudice.

Nation needed to keep the
colorful tapestry of human history
and ingenuity of culture and languages.

Borders of Nurture and Bonding
Not of Dominance and Bombing.
Bonding not Bombing – Please

———•••••———

An old bus
A bootlegger's mess

Bullets fly
The bottlers die

The intoxicating spirit
Soaks the greedy earth.

iii
~ *Bootlegger's Bus*

———•••••———

cannons of blood and gore
canons of love and joy
to make the bloody ones silent
to make the ageless silence Boom

Clubs have been raised
To crush skulls and snuff life
When viking heroes played their deadly game.

Time to defang the killer instinct
To play a lively game of love and life.

MANDELA

Man 'O' Man
He refused to surrender
The human in him even to the most inhuman
No matter what you take from him
You could not make him a lesser Man

Born of bondage and suppression
of the worst kind. Unrelenting
in his longing for Dignity and Freedom
Lived to see demonic rule end
Unfettered by bitterness or hate
Celebrating freedom with laughter and joy

Not many a man were born
Like him till our times
Hope he spawns many
Who will live like him.
The future needs many like him

Man 'O' Man

—— ••••• ——

Whatever the number of wheels
Rolling on without respite.
Don't you be crippled by impediments
Just roll on lovingly, joyfully.

—— ••••• ——

Camera can capture the lines on
the face, but who shall be able
to read the pains and pleasures,
joys and miseries above all the
depth of one's experience of life

A Picture

Does canvas and paint
make a picture
Or is it the hand and mind
that makes pictures

Or is it that pictures have always been
and you just find some

Lines and colors only
unveil the hidden folds
of human unconsciousness

The innards of mental structures
Not always a pretty picture

Vain Conquest

Our interest in Mars or Venus
is not of Curiosity or Love
but of senseless Greed and Conquest
It is not about Venus or Mars
but of endless need for more and more
This borderless Ignorance
cannot be satiated with more
The nature of who you are
Needs all and not more
All is yours as it is
If you include and embrace
This you will not know either
by Curiosity or Conquest

The School

Go to school to become a cog
Or go to school to know the fool
who refuses to become a cog or a
quaking frog

But to know the way to know,
as to know is to grow
To grow not to social or scriptural
prescriptions but to become Me, Myself
and what is beyond Me

With due respect to cogs and frogs
Don't you want to be something...
Something more than the more?

Reading

To read
Is to knead

A blockhead
Into a fountainhead

To know life profound
Before yours unfold

To know
All that you behold
Has been told

So be bold
Plunge into the old

As the unborn has a bond
With the long dead

Unnourished by the knowing of the dead
Will fashion yourself into a deadly dud.

To read
Is to knead.

———•••••———

Education is just about organizing this natural
longing to know and expand horizons.

———•••••———

Learning is not about earning
But a way of flowering

———•••••———

Technologies of today and
Tomorrow are but mere toys.
Play as you wish, knowing
the greatest worth of life is Within.

Rivers of Ink

Rivers of many hues
flow to nourish and alter
the course of lives upon the
planet. So does ink of
many a hue flow to alter,
nourish and corrupt minds
with Heaven–hell, Good–bad,
Superior–inferior, You–Me.
Every conceivable divide that
the maker of the worlds could
not conceive in his infinite will.

———•••••———

The Ancients laboured hard
to leave their footprint in edifice
of stone that lay waste with ravages
of Time. So shall all labours of Human be

———•••••———

From donkey carts to tillers
Vehicles change but the same toilers
These toilers someone wants to rule
Temporal or spiritual, but they have to toil.

———•••••———

In kicking a ball
There is much to realize.
Unless you do it right
It shall not happen.
No prayer or divine hand
Just the right kick.

———•••••———

The unkind ball has no
respect nor regard. Just
goes by the law, no allowance
no matter who you are.
So everyone needs a game

Cricket

Nation's passions aroused
A game has taken on
Gladiatorial proportions
A hard ball and gentle Willow
A billion people with many
of their hopes and aspirations
unfulfilled. But banking
on eleven men for pride
and glory. Down under are
many in their lives of poverty
and deprivation. Hoping in
great fervour that their cup of
Joy will come from Down Under.
The passion that unites a Nation
of incredible diversity

Poverty

In Poverty one achieves
a Perfection of suffering
that not even a deadly
ailment can do. In Poverty
Suffering endures like an
undiagnosed cancer
sapping you of all strength.
Molesting you with hunger,
debilitating and stripping you
of all dignity that every Human
strives to have.
One deadly scrounge that
we have failed to heal.

In times of Plenty, Poverty rules

———•••••———

All spiritual talk is vulgar
When our little child is in hunger

If you have known a moment of oneness
How could your heart remain in this weariness.

———•••••———

Lines drawn by humans should raze
To avoid hapless beings caught in a maze
Unmaking life from being a daunting daze

Could end all this in one loving embrace.

Migrants

They work with their Hands.
Heart breaking way of Urban
unconcern is new to these
sons and daughters of soil.
The native soil, language and
food. All that is familiar and
they loved deprived by the
longing to undo the grip of
Poverty. Moving away from
the comfort of a meager Home
and Hearth. Having buried
their Hearts in the village and
toiling in Urban unfamiliarity.
Uprooted but Hopeful lives
Now with upended Hope...

Shameless

A Peacock with his magnificent
plume, a masterpiece of color
and form without compare.
Has to let out high pitched calls
to get attention to his
immense Beauty.

Living in this world that is
distracted beyond words and
clueless of the many rewards
of keenness of attention.

In Challenging times that we are
If you have something of value
that could benefit life in smallest
ways. Stand up and shout
Shamelessly

———•••••———

To Touch and Transform
another life is all
there is to Human Action.

———•••••———

The joy of action is known
only to the one who has
no need for action.

———•••••———

Brawn or Brain
Needs relentless effort
to get to a place of
Significant Impact.

———•••••———

Pandemic

Are we making too much noise
So we cannot even hear ourselves
Have we reached such states of fakery
that our insulation to the truth of life
is just ceaseless Pandemonium.

A Pandemic of Pandemonium

Ticketless

As Railways begin to rattle
across this ancient Nation again.
Transporting and connecting its millions
the invisible invader salivates and lusts
for a free ride to the Billion of his desire.

It is for you to either provide incubation
for the invisible invader or deny in self isolation

~ In reference to the virus pandemic of 2020

Lockup

Do you need to be locked down
or do you possess the needed sense
to sanitize, distance and disinfect.
Are you in appreciation of those who
strive for you or are you
a lout with vulgar entitlements
or a religious nut who can
only live well in a Paradise
elsewhere. If you have no
sensitivity to appreciate
the dedication, commitment
and selflessness with which
Doctors, Nurses, Police and
even most Politicians are striving
to save your life and Mine
What you need is not lockdown
Lockup

Scarecrow

Once I met a scarecrow
And said "It must be tedious
Just to stand rooted and lonely"

Scarecrow replied "You do not
Know the joys of scaring, do you"

With my whiskers and wild beard
Should not take much to scare

Scarecrow replied "No, no. Only
those who are stuffed with straw
Can know the joy of scaring"

Stuffed with straw
Can you ever be a draw
And know the joys of sharing

Supreme Company

To be in the company of a Dummy
is life-consuming and nothing funny

Let no one be in dim company
As in just turning inward
there is supreme company

———·····———

Neither matted locks nor shaven head
Pulling hair one by one nor wearing ocher robes
Fools will know nothing by costume
Bereft of the inner knowing

At the most fill their bellies

Silence

Speaking and gaping
Your mouth will fill with dust
Watching others' fruits,
Yours will be eaten.

———•••••———

How can you speak of the ocean
to the frog in the well
Or of ultimate reality
to a thinking fool.

Transcendence

Dragon fly struggles
To go through the transparence of the glass
Eyes say this is the way to go
But even the gentle breeze does not pass
Ocular deception
So the transparent mind
Seems to let everything in
But nothing gets in or out
Clear the transparence
Deepen the Deception
By the bed side I find
the Dragon fly dead and dry.

———•••••———

Corridors of life
can take you round
and round unless
you stop and ponder.

———•••••———

Whatever mask you may choose
Your true nature you will lose.

Baggage-Free

There are doors of opportunities and possibilities
And there are doors of deeper perceptions
In opening doors of opportunity
You shall access new ways to live
In opening doors of perception
You shall experience richness of creation
Through opportunities you may gather
riches of wealth, comfort and recognition
Through perception unpeeled, you know
the nature of creation and the source.

Doors of opportunity shall make you
toil for a pittance that is made to
seem humungous due to the sufferings
of lesser men. By the time you
gather enough it is time for
baggage-free journey of mortality.

The doors of perception shall
get you nothing, but leave you
with a richness of your being that
makes nothing worthy of accumulation.

Baggage-free and ready for
journey of Life and Death.

Untouchable

There is a land that is
beyond right and wrong

When you get to that land
and lie there
humans who live for bread
and toil to be what they are not
will strive to hide their jealousy
with mocking talk
and the gods will descend to be
in the company they wish to be

Once you have reached that land
beyond right and wrong, you never have to worry about
making a mistake or going wrong

NATURE

Earth Sense

There is no match for her
Beauty nor her Brilliance.
Off her simple sod she bears
You and Me and all the
multifarious life forms of most
incredible form and hue.
If we did imbibe her sense
We would all be geniuses of the
most fantabulous sort.
We are just pop-ups upon her
generous Breast. We are borne
and nourished through our lives
only upon her Breast. In losing
conscious connection with her
We have lost our life.
The umbilical touch of breath
and bread taken for granted.
Never should you forget
She is the womb and of course
the Tomb.

The leaf

Wind moves as per
its call
The leaves rustle
ever so gentle
Causing the music of the
mute
The greenness of these leaves
did fly in the parakeet's glee
The sweetness did penetrate
the hardy cane of sugar
The hardness of Sun's fury
She tamed into life enhancing
flower, fruit and shade
And made light alluring
to man and beast alike
O' her charm and grace

Hey' man how could you forsake
the Magic of the music of the mute

Are you there

Jasmine buds blossom
to the call of the brilliant morn
As if to ensure that the beauty of
the precariously positioned Shabnam [Dew drops]
is not missed during the day

As the Sun chooses to give respite
to the seemingly endless toil of the Man and the Worm
The Night Queen exudes her intoxicating
fragrance to compliment the translucence of the Moon

Day or Night the Mother Earth strives
to fill beauty and fragrance to our dreary lives

O' Man, are you there to taste, smell and see
the glory of the Sky, Land and Sea

Dirty little Logic

As flowers become fruits
with a touch of Magic Spring
Green leaves did become flowers
Brown branches became leaves
Knotted roots became a
Luxuriant tree exuding the
very Plasma of life.

All this from the soil
that some call – Dirt.
Is this a Dirty – Life
or the Magic of Creation
You shall know as per
your Incline.

Inclined to pay attention to the Magic of Creation
or engrossed in your own
Dirty little logic

Kaleidoscope

The green leaf
the lighter green leaf
much lighter green leaf
countless varieties of green leaf.
Who is the mad painter
and what brand of paint...
As I immerse myself in these
endless types of green leaves
I see the purpose to this madness
A purpose more insane than
the Kaleidoscope.

Geo

The shape of our mother
We do not know, unless
Inebriated with spirits
Or lost some fluids in our heads

She is on a spin perennial
Spinning and weaving our mortal coil

Is she not our potter's wheel
Steady, on course and even keel

Her breast of bounty is our sap
And her womb our tomb.

———·····———

The womb of the ocean
salty and pristine
is a reminder of a mother
beyond you, me and the other.

———·····———

Of you and me

The flower upon the tree,
The filth at its roots,
What do you know
Of filth and fragrance?

———·····———

Earth by her nourishment binds the tree
Sky by its light keeps setting it free

———·····———

Aerodynamic

Harvesting the winds
For the joy of finding wings
Wherever we are
It is time to reach out
and touch the Sky.

Clouds

The Lenticulars and the
Cumulus. The fat fluffy ones
and the thin sheer. The Dark
rain bearing ones and the
purposeless white ones. Some
saw them as symbols of gloom
and some as the shape of life.
Will you stop naming and judging
and just enjoy the geometry
of their forms

Fluff

Fluffy plumes of Cloud
have no clue that they
are holding up the precious
water and light from
the parched, dark land.

Ignorance is not aware
that it is obscuring the
Spectacular possibility of
Enlightenment. Innocence
is not in the know that
the fluff of life is the
Dark cloud that is a
Possibility but not yet.

Substanceless fluff should
not deny you the
greatest of all Possibilities.

love affair

Monsoon, breeze gentle
with sweet coolness that
hides the fury that you shall
unleash in days and weeks to come
A fury welcomed by the parched
land and life, except for that lazy
Ant that failed to get back into
its mound quick enough.
I can smell the fury and my
body trembles in expectation
of this Visitation of
Year on Year love affair.

Earth flavor

When the monsoon winds
drive heavy with earthy smells

The mortal coil – an earthen pot
trembles to the flavor of Life and Death

These bones and sinews, this heart and liver,
the genital jewel and the cerebral flower

All just earth, touched by the Divine Source
enshrined in the innards of this earthy edifice

To know this earthy mould will not suffice
as it flourishes but for a trice

Rise, beyond Life and Death
upon my grace enthroned

Oh' Soil

The fragrance of the Soil
Somehow is more tenderness
to Me than the fancy
fragrance of the Flower.

The strength and sensitivity
of life held in the Soil lets
off waves of passion of a
different sort. Passion not
of a person but of my
species that has gone insensitive
to all that nurtures it
and absorbs it at its end.
As I walk barefoot, I break down
with Passions so profound
that it defies all descriptions.

Oh' Soil, My life

Lilt

To lay under a tree
On a hot summer afternoon
Fruit flies buzz lazily.
The flutter of the butterfly
has slowed to match the mood.
A lazy tropical summer afternoon.
Gazing up at the magic of
exquisite geometry of branches,
twigs, leaves and above all
the enterprising rays of Sun finding
their way through this magical mess.
My innards tingle with rapture
of pure life and willingness to
merge into the very sod
that I lay upon

SOIL

The Soil that you walk upon
The Soil that you treat as Dirt
Is the Magical material
that turns into leaf, flower
and fruit. All that you
know as life was at one time
held in the eternal pregnancy
of the Sacred Soil. Mother
to some and Dirt to some other.

But the Sacred Source of all

The life encasing cage
of the body is but the Soil.

Under farmer's Till, potter's
Wheel, above all the Divine Will
It turns into Magical Mill

Conscious Planet

My Body, Your Body
Every Body is Bonded
to the Earth Body,
The Very Soil we walk upon
We bear as our Body.
Shall we come awake to
Strengthen the Soil, Strengthen
Our bodies, Strengthen all life
and above all leave
Rich Sod for the Unborn.
Let us not forget we are
Only a link in the Chain
of Humanity in this Eternity.
You, Me and Everyone Come awake
Come awake, Come awake.

Soul Snare

The body that you wear
Many before you did wear

The soil that Mother Earth wears
Is something that we all share

The body that you wear and care
Is only good as soul snare

Do you have enough dare
To release Self from soil's care?

From earth we seep
and shall seep back to earth
In between, if restfulness
is your mode of action
Blessed you are, Blessed you are.

Elements

With just five
a magnificent hive
All of nature's bounty
Just elemental mischief.

3rd Quarter

Spring time mist hovers and
tingles my naked skin raising
pimples of the birdy sort.

Peacock calls hours later than his
3rd Quarter call, looks a bit hazed out
by mist. Been up for hours, letting my
body go cold. One of those days when
Timeless longings from another time led
to a life of austerities harsher than
Nature's prescriptions, surface.

Hunger, Cold, Pain, but the
unquenchable fire of longing
for dimensions that no more
elude me. But not to forget
the pain of not knowing
that led to all this...

Mist

Misty morning brings
a certain mingle. Makes
Sky and Earth tango
Erases the border lines
of who is who and what
is what. The magic of Mist
gets all into a Mingle

Summer Rain

The dark and puffy faced cloud
looks like ready to cry, cry he must

Sheds his tears to unburden and be light
The grounded life sings and dances in delight

Every blessed drop a source of life.

Summer

Fragrance of flowers
keeping bees and birds
busy and Happy.

Crickets going jeee
day and night about
something they gained or lost.

Breeze ever so hesitant, either
to spread the coolness it carries
or hold it to itself.

You can be fragrance or filth
Can lose or gain
Share or Shed

Buzz of a Bee

In the buzz of a bee I heard the raga
And the meaning of Life
And the longing for The Beyond
The buzz of the bee wakes me up from a
slumber of a thousand years
Eons of lethargy dissolved and landed upon
the sweetness of a
flower

Cicada

An orchestral chorus of Cicada
Ceaseless in their musical
enthusiasm that dismisses such
trivia as monotony. Through
the Day and the Night their
Unceasing industry make
them almost Human. Trees are
heavy with their Millions, unconcerned
in their discordant plunder.

Me searching for an evolutionary
Distance between Cicada and Man

Frogy World

A tiny frog croaks and leaps
in ungainly haste upon the
porch. As I wonder what ordained
purpose he is out to fulfill.

What frogy business or profession
drives him. Maybe in feverish hurry
to his market or exchange. Or he
may be the leader of a frog democracy
or a monarch rushing to the Parliament
or Court. But he is alone no courtiers
or sidekicks that cannot be even in the
frogy world. One with such a
significant Voice must be of some
importance – Maybe a spiritual
leader or a religious head.
Or is he a cursed Prince waiting
to be kissed by a lovely maiden.

Mr. frog sets me off into seemingly
endless pursuit of finding purpose
for a frogy frog – croak croak

King Cobra

Swaying and slithering
he weaves a magic of his own
Deadly as he has become
still the choice of the Divine.

What hand or eye could
come up with this perfection
and poison all crafted into
this magical being. His courtship
is legendary, his venom
an instant relief from life.
Adam's lure but a yogi's allure
His mesmeric gaze could be
an invitation to Life or Death.

Your venom has cured me of Life
Your venom saved me from Death
Above all, your venom did dissolve my Ignorance
You have been fatal to my love and life
But can I ever help adoring you.

Serpents

Most maligned creatures in all of divine creation.
These gentle, colorful beings to me have not only
been dear but defining.

———•••••———

Tiger mask, lion mask.
Monkey mask, donkey mask.

Man mask, woman mask.
Divine. Only if you unmask.

Of Dogs and Cats and Pigs and Rats

Of dogs and cats and pigs
and rats, who is supreme?

There are those who bark and bite
their tools are made of fear
Fear keeps everything in order
The virtues of fear are too many to list
It can even render you short of breath
and short of everything that is life
Fear is living death

There are those who puss and purr
Sleek and soft full of inducements
For whom life is a seduction
A sweet poison of the marketmen
Tying you up not in chains but in silks
Entangling you in ways
That does not leave you any way

There are those who grunt
and of course stink. To get
the right kind of grunt you
have to bend and snivel and give
something to ingest. Their official sty
is a place you dread but there
is no way you can avoid this slime

There are those who nibble
at all that is yours. There is no
sanctity for your bridal dress or
your long departed grandmother's
What you worship they will work at
Nothing remains unexplored, they could
even invade your soul. O' soulmates

Of dogs and cats and pigs and rats
O' the evolutionary haste.

King of the jungle.
There isn't a whiff of majestic scent,
just hunger pangs and bad breath.

———·····———

The Animal in you
if you tame
The Human in you shall
not cringe or crouch

The Animal outside we have tamed
It is the Animal within that is a challenge
Much courage it takes to castrate the Bull within.
Only in taming the Animal past, lies the Divine future.

Revolution

Evolution seems like an
infinitely lazy process
For a mind that is in haste

All that is grand and Beautiful
a consequence of evolution
Including the super hasty Us.
Humans in haste are turning
everything into mountains of waste.

Time to stop the mindless haste
and look at the magic of evolution
where there is nothing that goes waste.

Revolution is a quick turnaround
that inevitably gets you back
to the very place that you started.

If there is keenness of attention
Evolution the greatest Revolution

Pepper

In the spice mountain
the hot stuff did grow
on cool green vines
These hot corns did
Set the European tongues
aflame, that they crossed braving
wild uncharted oceans
Just to have a taste of
the Hot stuff.
The green beads that turn
into black gold brought
invaders that laid waste
the Orient Sanctity of the
land of Mystics & Saints.

Fire

Many
manifestations of fire

An element that you
love and fear

The controlled fires of
hearth and heart.

The fires that sustain
and comfort

Then the fires that
propel and drive us

In turbines, engines
and motors

And of course the more
intimate fires

of digestion, regeneration
and imagination

In our belly, groin
and brain.

All of it, inspired by
the solar fire

from the sun above

In managing these fires
is our well-being

In losing control,
is our nemesis

Global Warming

Fire on the mountain

In the darkness of the night
Pretty it stands like jewel among starlight

How destructive can
This pretty be

Many a creature must be burning
Death in untold agony

It is the distance that
Makes even destruction so pretty

If you distance yourself
From this body and all

Indestructible you will be

So you see how the destroyer
Shiva, the taintless one
Became the great Lord

Forest Flower

A flower that is unconcerned
About attention or appreciation
Shall for always blossom
And spread fragrance unheeded

———·····———

Orchid Blossom

The orchid blossom
just stares me in the eye
Me just stares back at
the matchless wonder

Confounded

Rocks and more Rocks
not just lying there but
have risen to impossible
geometric symphony.

Staring down at you like
living things, that they are.
What insane Heart and
industrious Hand could
put them all up in these
Magnificent forms the
human eye finds hard
to comprehend, all one can
do is, stare Confounded.

Confounded by this Craft
of Creation

~ At Arches National Park

Terra

In the cold mountains
She in a state of steamy
passion. She is not a wench
blowing hot or cold but of
motherly warmth and womb.

Of Hail and Rain

Rain for the Parched Tongue
Hail for the Blocked Head

Hail and Rain True Magic from the Sky

Rain the Nourishing Bosom
Hail the Crushing Reason

Of Hail and Rain
There is Pain and Gain

Are You Ready for the Kneading
That Will Bring You to Blessed Knowing

Are You Willing to Shed Familiar You
To Know the Blissed Void that is Me

Monsoon

Pouring rain and red earth
meet and mingle like lovers
Passion crazed in feverish haze
With the single mindedness
to end all that is oneself
To merge and know the other.
This longing to destroy oneself
And to be delivered into the other.

What immortal hand did put them apart
Only to be put together as mortal pawns

Red earth and pouring rain
have met indeed not to lie as slush
To nourish life to life and keep dead – dead.
To become tree, flower or fruit
When this earth & sky kiss & copulate
This earth with life will populate
It is in this life that Divine celebrates.

Monsoon

As monsoon rains lash
sometimes furious, at times gentle
big blobby drops that could hurt
or fine needle spray – enchanting
puddles of water upon the mud tracks
Trees and plants seem to be boiling
in joy, moving with the wind or moving the winds
at times furious or just still
Dance of life and life making material
How well orchestrated these two months are
will determine the life for the coming year
for all the creatures including humans
in this part of the world. Monsoon this
time around not soon enough. Many
an anxious eye scanning the skies
to see and receive the lively dance of life.

Monsoon

Ah, what a boon

Parched earth receives
like a lost lover.
It is never too soon.

All creatures in a silent
celebration. When it gets
heavy and takes a toll
we bow in respect but never
resist. No one to mourn
those who die of flood
as we have been saved
from the ravage of famine.
The blessed drops descend
to seemingly impregnate
our mother's already seeded womb.

No hormone nor steroid
did inspire such spurt of growth.

Ah, monsoon – never too soon

Mist

Valley obscured by the veil
of mist so fragile
Human prejudice would brood
of foreboding prospects
with vision impaired the
cerebral overdrive begins
to paint pictures of gloom

Me step into this misty embrace
the cool warmth of womby
murkiness. Me notice the leaves
dripping their orgasmic drip.
Birds and insects wet with
pleasure. Me close my eyes
Knowing and sharing this
Misty ecstatic Drip

Aadi

These winds that roar
down the mountainscape

This is the time for
Wind washing this sacred mount.

All that is rigid is flattened
to the ground and only those
who are willing to bow will
survive this Abhishekam by
the wind gods. If you are
close to the bosom of the mother
Earth you will remain. If you
stick out you shall be blown away
and broken, smashed to smithereens.

These winds having touched
my Master's feet spread across
the Deccan to spread his grace.

Having prepared this land with
rich Grace, now is there a choice
of sowing the potent
seed? The seed will be dispersed
to touch and transform all in this
hoary peninsula.

*~ Aadi is the Tamil month that falls in July-August; the windy season,
pre-monsoon winds.*

Autumn

As I kissed the Autumnal sky
with a passion, a full blooded
Woman would long for in her
inevitable lonely nights that
associates with long lost Beloved.

The colours change in a
serious blush that can not
escape even the sightless eyes
of the blind. The leafy panels fall
with their job done, making way
for a seasonal death or a
moult with which life takes
a break from daily chores of
harvesting light, air and food.
From the mundane chores to
a seemingly ascetic stillness.
A break from life but not in death
A break from life to spring back
to renewed life of leaf, flowers and fruit.

Fall Time

Leaves of every hue
colourful feast for eye
But a death dance
of colour. Not of gaiety
but of cold gravity
Crown and clothing
all tumbling down
Being stripped off
of life making sap
Trees will stand naked
of leaf, flower or fruit
Only in hope of
another lease of life
Autumnal fall
Winter's rot
Spring's surprise
This not of life or death
but of life and death
Not a catastrophe
But a carnival
No where to go
As all is Here.

The Leaf

After the final colorful
Dance of the fall time.
Falling away gracefully
to carpet the land
in numberless hues
Waiting for the snows
to turn the Sap into Sod
A willing participant in
the life process of
Recycle

...fall guy

As snowflakes descend
gently to put much life
to much needed Rest.
A layer of fallen leaf
begins to hatch a secret
sauce under cover of the
white Blanket, to regenerate
life for a fresh start.
The falling of the leaf
if you thought was a pity
was only playing the fall
guy to become nourishment
to Rise to the pinnacle of
the Treetops scraping the skies

Seasons of Slumber

Though the flowerless winter
makes the Sun sad, denied
of colourful reception. Still
chooses to shine bright as
he knows that he is the source
of the leaf and the flower.
Colour and colourlessness are
just features of the passing season
like the sweetness of life is devoid of reason.
Bare and cold only lie in preparation
for the bright and warm spring.
As leaf and flower shall spring
back from their seasonal slumber,
One who shines through the winter
shall for sure find flower and fruit.

The very bareness shall blossom.
Succumb not to seasons of slumber.

Of Snowflakes and Me

The snowflakes white and light
They say are falling heavy tonight

As I walk with an upturned face
To receive their fragile grace

Me wonder if the heaven is falling apart
Or just in a flaky freakout

Must be heavens falling out
To spring back at spring

Me a snowflake too
As fragile and grace

If you have an upturned face
Me fall to spring back in heaven's grace

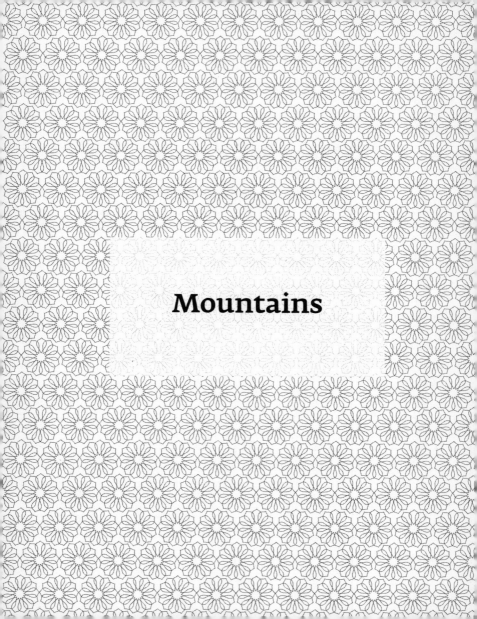

Mountains

ANNAPURNA
(Goddess of Nourishment)

Tall and majestic
Dressed in white
Like an angel
But pitiless and bare
As a devil
She is mesmerizingly beautiful
Nourishes the world
by her melting whiteness
dripping down into tumultuous streams
and great rivers
the giver of all important nourishment
Annapurna.

~ Kalopani, Nepal, See You Resort, 2:30 AM

Annapurna means one who gives you food.
This mountain feeds so many rivers,
and rivers are the basis of food for most human beings.

LIKE YOU AND ME

Of mountains and valleys
Of trees and rocks
Even the white cloud
And the river
Each an extension of the other
Pretending to be different
Just like you and me.

MOUNTAIN LACE

Snows melt to cover
the bare mountain face
with the white lace of streams
large or rills thin and
sinuous. This fragile
lace of white water
turns into torrential river
that all shall fear and respect

ANNAPOORNA

Snow clad peak of
Annapoorna revealing its
fair face for a moment and
going behind the veil of cloud
the next playing the shy bride
forever. Until the photon force
of the Sun momentarily unveils her
Glorious face to enthrall all
momentarily though.

the trek

Mountain Air
makes me flare
Gets my old bones dare
to romp and climb
the heartless rocks
that leave me mauled and bare

~ Kalopani, Nepal, See You Resort, 1:40 AM

Mountains are such a pain
Upon your knees and wear you down
But the exhilaration and joy that they bring
makes it all a dizzy rapture.

Mountains are a measure of a Man
How tiny, puny and insignificant.
How gusty, resilient and indomitable
Mountains can make or Break you.

Painful Paradise

Overshadowed by
the snowy Annapurna

The beautiful Manang
valley and my mountain
madness, intoxication of
oxygen deficient chill air

The promise of stretching
every muscle fiber into
a painful paradise

It is not in search
of ultimate liberation
that I make this journey

It is just the pleasure of
pure air, pain and the test of pluck

It is the mountain, its mist
and mystique. Above all
my madness that sets off
a magical tingle in all that
is Me and the Mindless
Sense of heady Emptiness

Journey to Muktinath I walk
unfettered by life or death

Blissful Burden

My Heart beats best
when among Mountains.
My Body does protest
But I cannot be Unmountained
for too long. My ruthless
Master invested the burden
Of a Mountain in Me.
I try hard to settle
At the foothills but my
Heart longs for Mountain
Peaks. What would I be
without the Blissful Burden.

...foot hills

We chose the foothills to live
and the mountain top to die.

Who wants to keep this animal (body)
When we reach the top peak.

An insult to the lord
to offer this flesh that rots.

Shambho when I come –
I come without this (body)

To Kailash

Like the snows, I come and go
Like the snows, I melt at your feet
Like the snows, I adorn you
I am your footwear and your crown
Just trying to be as much to you
As you are to me

Will not only keep coming to you
As long as my lungs can hold
this life breath and my legs can hold
up to the pressures exerted by
the embrace of my Mother – Earth

Don't you mistake my southern
origins for the arrogance of
the ten-headed Lankan king

With my sheer absence
I will hold and transport you
South of Vindhyas. As the
ancient people of these gentle
lands have longed for You
for too long. Steadfast in devotion
Their hearts throb with
One single emotion
for You, You and You

Manasarovar

Inviting ripple of the
Blue waters hold intrigues
of unfathomable sort.

Its profound depths have
been flirting with me but
I remained aloof to
its wooing not knowing
if I can grasp what is
hidden in its pristine blue
or could become absorbed
into its allure and depths.

The tease of the unknown
is magnetic, but am I dealing
with the Unknown or the Unknowable.

Purposeless

Layers of mountains
mesmerizing in their misty mystique
Sit there lazy and purposeless
Home and nourishment to much life
But stoic in purposeless stillness

———·····———

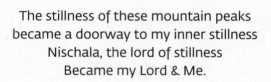

The stillness of these mountain peaks
became a doorway to my inner stillness
Nischala, the lord of stillness
Became my Lord & Me.

———·····———

This affair with the mountains
Is not just a frivolous fare

A reminder of a profound fare
Of lifetimes of longing and an eternal affair

Kailash

A glorious being of immense
proportions, when longed
to share his monumental
knowing. Found all seekers
Inadequate and unable
to receive this torrent of
ceaseless knowledge. Of all
there is and all that isn't.
A knowing that encompasses
every manifestation of
creation, its innards and
the very basis of all there is.
Unable to find a seeker
of the right magnitude
chose this Sacred Rock
May no fool treat this
as just another Rock
to languish in ignorance
forever. Let all know
this Rock is a choice
above all Beings.

Himalaya

Even the rocks reach out to the heavens.
No wonder beings seeking divine
made you their abode

You, of gushing waters and rushing airs
towering presence of unsurpassable grace

The brave hands that crafted these paths
into your ceaseless folds:
a mighty effort, but miniscule

Many have traveled this labyrinth
that seemingly leads to your very womb

The womb that the courageous ones sought
to die and be born once again

These Dwijas – the twice born
of immeasurable wisdom
Left imprints that even
the final deluge can erase not

O deathless ones, your energies and wisdom
here lives through me
I have the keys to your grace and boundlessness.

Every beating heart claims to seek
As I peel to reveal
The weak-hearted ones run
to save their frailties
But a few lusty ones remain

Lust – lust for life – deeper life
is the only way to unravel
the bounty of nothingness
that is me and you

—— ••••• ——

The Himalayan chill
Does remind you that you are mortal

When the chill touches your bones
Burn we must either wood or the Bone.

—— ••••• ——

Velliangiri's lap has been more than my mother's
for many lives has kept me nurtured and
above all focused upon my master's will.

Velliangiri

The ceaseless flow
of the silvery brook
hurrying on like it is
on a fretful mission

The surrounding forest
in its drooping silence stands
nourished and mesmerized
by this liquid roar

If there is a place that could heal
a traumatized heart,
this should be the best
among treatments of all sorts

A tranquil mind and a loving heart
a fiery pride and gentle act
is all a possibility
in this idyllic space

Rivers

Life Line

O' rivers the very juice
of my life. The basis of
our civilizations. Your liquid
Magic we turned into our
Bodies. O' rivers you sustained
All life with your liquid flourish
Crisscrossing Bharat like the
arteries of nourishment making
blood and body of the Nation
We shall commit to protecting
you not only of love but greed
that our progeny shall sustain
In this Sacred Sod.

Mother Cauvery

Mother Cauvery, I am the child in your lap
I bit the very breast that fed me
You are the way for my life and liberation
I grew up in your lap
The fool that I am, kicked the Mother herself
Forgive this life of a fool
We have ruined the life of the yet to be born
You are the very blood in my veins
I offer my life to you
Mother Cauvery

O' Rivers

Not only from birth to death I need you
Even after death I need you
to submerge my ashes
O' Rivers...you must flow

We humans have
dammed you, jammed you
and dug holes into you
Allow me to nourish you

O' Rivers
We can never pay back the debt
for all that you have done to us
Let me at least pay a small interest
towards your well-being

— ••••• —

It is for You and Me
To keep waters flowing
To Him and Her who are yet to be.
For all life let waters flow.

— ••••• —

A Body of water that
invigorates life can be a lake
so sacred or just a slice of fruit.
Many ways of the life giving water

Precarious as it seems
to cross a river in a fragile
dingy. There is no real danger
here. If you succeed you
get to the other bank, if you
don't you get to the Ocean

Blue Nile

Defying the harshest desert
nurtured the birth and growth
of a stupendous human effort

The indomitable writ
of the pharaoic era
A monumental stamp
of the Egyptian spirit

Blue Nile cuts through
the desolate Saharan sands
like maternal passage promising life,
Life that is and Life to be.

Vast ruthless desert
the cool Blue Nile, a combination
that bred a culture sublime.

INTELLIGENT IDIOTS

A civilization cultured by
the River. The River revered
as flowing from the head
of the Great lord. The River
that can cleanse and nourish.
The River that is source of
salvation for the dead and
liberation for the living.
We have contaminated and
contained. Choked and
maimed. Time to look
at not how to exploit
but to nourish and preserve.
This is not being an eco-warrior
but the formula for sustenance
and survival of the most
intelligent idiots that we are.

Sun, Moon
and Stars

The Sun

The Brown Earth
A green Leaf
A colorful Butterfly
Soft sounds of a Bird
Cloudless blue Sky
All the magic of the
Pristine Light

No matter...

As clouds spread to
sunscreen the planet,
to long for the warmth
of the Burning Ball.

Unconcerned he burns
and does not suffer
lack of attention from
all life that thrive
fed upon his indomitable
fire of light and warmth.

Let not you wait for
reception of the right sort
May you Burn Bright
No matter, world looks your way or Not.

Cycles

All that is physical
Are products of cycles
Cycles of the Moon
Cycles of our Beloved Mothers

Cycles of Heat and Cold
Cycles of Air and Water
Cycles of Rivers and Oceans
Cycles of Solar and Lunar
Above all the consequence of karmic cycles

All cycles are about going in circles
Of going round and round

Need for being in the familiar
Keeps one in the swoon of cycles

Seemingly eternal nature of this spin job
Can only be broken by clearing
the inebriation of the cyclical
By striving in Guru's Grace.

Either Or

Of the Sun and the Moon
Who is more important?

Of course the Sun
Says reason

The moon faced dreamer
Ponders and sings praise of the Moon

What a contest betwixt the fiery source of light
And the waxing and waning nightly delight

Thus arises the grosser question
Who is superior the man or woman

Then a mind lost in the logical bareness
Raises these questions of senselessness

Upon assumed elevation of religious loft
Asks – Of the Creator and Creation which is paramount

In this Either Or
You can know neither this nor that

A mind which has chosen to fragment
Is the source of all human torment

Everything is in absolute embrace of Everything else
A futile mind which attempts to fragment the existence

This mind the only barrier to cross
To reach the peak of Enlightenment
from the depths of ignorance

The only debacle
But the only vehicle

Make this treacherous journey
Or simply rest in Me.

Of Leadership

When the Starlings fly in
their Collective Glory, can
anyone decipher the leader of
their magnificent act

The Heart beats, Glands secrete,
Kidneys purify, every cell performs
the most exacting functions
and the Brain reflects

The many Billion Galaxies
of effervescent stars and nascent
space. Of Black holes and
Milky Ways, does someone see
a Center that leads

A leader is a Fool

Solstice

To see winter's mist
collapsing into itself
Exposing the valley
like a guileless Bride.

All that could have been
green or many hued wonder
of the fall has turned gray
With passover of Solstice done
Much warmth and light
Is coming our way

Sun Beams

Sun Beams kept rolling
down through the dormers
Diagonals were their choice
of descent and design.

Meaningless designs of
patterns impossible, a phenomenon
untarnished by meanings.

leaves me empty and silent

Sun within

In the absence of Sunlight
Dark clouds & dark moods of nature
Everything silent except the automobile.

I the truly motherless one
never did grow basking in the sun without
The warmth and light never from outside

Everyone seems to bake from outside.
But not I
Only from within was I baked
May be that is why the right shade

~ In reaction to a comment on my complexion

It is You

When the sky is gray
The grieving clouds forget
That they themselves
Have blotted the Sun out

————•••••————

Though many faces of the moon
Have beauty and significance of their own
It is the full moon that quenches the thirst
and raises the oceans.
Look for the revelation of the Mystic face.

MOON

Your varying geometry a cause
of concern, as the oceans slosh
and humans of the menstrual sort
grapple with Passion and manic Moods.
As if desperate to find the missing
form of that day and longing for
your fullness. After a day of deception
the Moony Madness relaunches itself
for our Birth.

Mystic Moon

Fairy-taled to believe
that you are a ball of Butter.
Then made to believe that someone
stepped upon you and a giant
leap for Mankind. All those
lonely nights spent gazing
at your varying geometry,
wondering what you are made
of and how you are engaged
in my making. Making
of my Body and the orbit
of my perception
Just when I was about
to figure, you changed shape
to be more elusive to my eye blinded
by the fallacy of light. Only when my
eye began to see Darkness empowered by
light within did I unveil the many secrets
of your changing form. Though only
a reflection you had the power to
manipulate the maternal fluids to
manage my Birth and thou shall
also have a hand in my Death.
You have been the
revolving Door to
my knowing.

The Moon

Embodying the raging madness
exuded by the Moon
Became the fountainhead
of unfathomed mysteries
hidden in the Moon

Ageless outpouring I became
of the coolness of the Moon.

My love's lust took in
the deadly venom
in the fullness of the Moon

Gave up another Beloved to merge into
the graceful light of the full Moon

If lord's grace be upon me,
will shed this coil
in the grandeur of the full Moon

SHIVA

Rudra (The Roarer)

With the first Roar
Galaxies fell out of your
Void. Here we scream
to throw out all that
checks and chokes us.

In a Roar you created
the limitless Creation of yours
In a Roar, we wish to destroy
the listless creation of ours.

Hoping our roars will resonate
with your mighty Roar of Creation.

Tear we did the chords of Sound
Open we did the doors of the
Profound.

May every wimpy sound we
make be in tune with your Roar.

Of Cymbals and Drums

A gleeful meeting of
Sound and silence
Becomes the 'Sundar Sangeet' (beautiful music)
Of Shiva's Thunderous dance.

Cymbals and drums
Poor cousins of my silence.
Have to beat them to get
Something out of them.

Shiva's silence can
Drip galaxies for free.
Oh yes there is space for
You, You and You too.

The power and beauty
Of this endless space.

Touch it with your song
Touch it with your dance
Touch it with your stillness
Even a scream will do.

Touch it and you
Will drip ecstasy.

Shiva Shiva

The Cosmic Vibrance
just a Divine din
The Bangs of Creation
that made galaxies galore
And the pangs that
gnaw at the gut and groin
All a process of
Creation and deception
The Sleight of the Divine
hand, revealing a side
and leaving the
other to be unraveled

The Cosmic din dominates
the human sense that
laps up this labyrinth
of sounds.
Those who seek may even
know the primordial.
But all will make the
prime possibility of
that which is Not.
They will know This, That,
Him and Her. Missing
Me and Shiva
Me and Me

UNVISIONED

The formless One
Takes a glorious form
Not of any intrinsic need
but of compassion for the Blind
who can only see the boundaries
of form, the limitations of light
The confines of knowledge.
Boundlessness
is only for the unvisioned – The Seer
of lightless, borderless, Shi-va

Linga

You are the firstborn
The first expression of the cosmic emptiness

The wise ones espied you
to be the source of all this lively mischief

You are the source of all pain and pleasure
You are the lowest and the highest

Ah, the games that you play!
The multitude of forms
for which you are the source
are neither this nor that

I wormed through creation
to discover you and me

O Ishana, the most glorious form!
Blessed is Isha to be your abode

The Glorious One

In your limitless abode you sit
like you are the very
center of the universe

All the loving hands that toiled to make
dome divine your domain
are blessed with blissful owners

As I enter this domain divine
for the thousandth time
my spine tingles with sensations
that a young lass wouldn't have dreamt of

Sensations that will melt
stony hearts to pulp
blaze dim beings into beings of light
transform weaklings into powerhouses

The wretched into virtuous
the joyless into blissful
raise cowards into the realm of the fearless

For the one who has known these
divine sensations of Dhyanalinga,
the glories of life will play at his feet

HIS ABODE - Adiyogi Alayam

You did not ask
for Devotion or Surrender

Your way was just to offer
free of all ritual and fetish

It is all just a question of
our gumption and absorption

You did not share what you know
but include into what you are

A tame-less being I see in you
lost all traction between me and you

My breath and my Being
Glad all are seeing

Dhyanalinga

You are my Guru's will
My only obsession
In my dreams and my wakefulness
My only longing was to fulfill you

Willing to do anything
That men should and should not
Willing to offer myself and
Another hundred lives if need be

Here now that you have happened
O' Glorious One
May your Glory and Grace
Stir the sleeping hordes
Into wakefulness and light

Now that you have happened
And the gift of life still with me
What shall I do with myself

Have lived the peaks for too long
Time to graze the valleys of life

What is man

O' Shambho what to say
of the power of Ignorance
A wisp of life called Man
who lingers in your lap
lives and dies by a puff of Breath
Says you are just stone
If you are stone what is man.

Invisible Delights

There are some
who climb the mountain peak

But there are those
who come down to the peak

What to say of our Shambho's
visible heights and invisible delights

Shiva Bond

Inspite of the venomous sting
The bee can only gather sweetness

Inspite of the deadly fangs
The cobra sits upon His brow

Inspite of the filth beneath
The lotus flower exudes fragrance

Inspite of limitless ignorance
I carry you as my crown

Can darkness extinguish light
Can ignorance eclipse knowing

In bonding with you
I have become boundless

Venomous Intent

O' Serpent king
You took my life when needed
But your venom brought me back
To life in a way, few would know
Whenever you appear my life turns a page
Now what do you have for me
That you have come
And it is time for the winds of change
I can still feel the venom
In my blood
Will I succeed in sieving
The chaff from the grain
The mortal from the Immortal

The serpent king
he can neither walk nor sing
but made his way to be Shiva's crown
the ignorant say he is devil's will
This 'me' made it to knowing
only by his venomous sting.

Kanti Sarovar

This peaceful abode of Shiva
a pool of grace in this wondrous space
it is here that I heard the sounds of grace.
Having been done with creation, his hands
he washed here, our Shiva.

Kailash

An eye

into the infinite lie
This stoic but profound stimuli

Is but a peep into the cosmic lie
Truth is only an impetus

to know the lie

That which is, is but a sham
That which is not is supreme
Who you are, an empty dream
That which you are not is life's cream

Cream, not of churning stream
But of all-consuming Shivam

Shiva

You drew two lines for everyone
Betwixt which to live their lives

But just one for me

To see that I don't cross YOU
I am willing to cross the whole creation

You made me in your own mould
Infused me with your fire

My longing and your will
To warm this world with your fire

But the warmth of your fires
Could burn the lifeless infidels

That they will name me the evil
And in turn YOU

Game of no returns

I prided in a heart
Strong and stable as a Rock
Then He came uninvited,
made my heart Beat and Bleed
For every Creature and the Rocks.

One hundred and twelve tricks
to beat the mortal coil
But trapped me in these tricks
The Wily One, now I am tricked
I can neither think nor do anything
that is for Me or of Me.

After having heard all the sweet sounds
After having seen all the Great sights
After knowing all the lovely sensations
I lost all my sense for Him, the One
Who is Not but IS like no other

He is not love
Nor is He compassion
Seek Him not for Comfort
For He is ultimate Fruition.

Come know the nameless
Ecstasies of the formless One
Not the joys of fulfillment
This is a game of Self Demise
Are you a sport for a game of No-returns

Don't you trust the Still One
He drew Me in with his Stillness
Me thought He was the way
Be warned He is the End.

Will you be there for
your funeral and the Grand
Cremation. The Fire Works
of the Cremation keeper. My Shiva

To Shiva

Like torrents of Ganga
tamed by your matted locks
The torrent of You flowing
down these sacred Hills
My Master tempered the flow
so that the human vermin are
not terrified by your Divine force.
The force that you are transformed
Into Grace

The Greatest and the only
privilege for me has been that you
have flown through me.
And flown through me to good effect.
The privilege
that you are graced upon me
I've strived to turn it into a
possibility for all.

May you have the sense
to keep the spout that
spouts nothing but you
in good form and trim.

Shambho

Unorthodox in thought, word and deed
The very stance they say is a sacrilegious deed

My breath and body an unencumbered slight
Encumbered minds believe must fight

As I am of him who is not of this world
Of him whose graceful expression is the world

A willfully bonded slave I am to him
Grateful to live by his every whim

Should you live and not know him
Futile is my life, what a shame.

Imbecile

O'Shambho
You made me yours
Setting a purpose and pitch
The guileless me fell for your charm
And took on much that is beyond me
When I saw that you were a little too much
I did apply you to the world
And the world was willing too
There is nothing here that is me or mine
Took everyone as mine as they were yours
This imbecile me has no will of my own
Let me not do that which would disgrace you
You chose me, you directed me, you set me forth
You chose to make this imbecile
Your lowly part

I have no will of my own
Make me your lowly part

My Love

Shambho for me is everything
My flirtations with everyone and everything
including my body
Only because I see Him in all.
My only love affair is Him.

This me is mad.
If you are clever choose now.
If you are a Fool for the love-Divine
There is nowhere else to go.
Come dissolve into me.

One and the Same

The transparence of the morn'
carries the fragrances of the birds
chirping crystal clear!

What secrets they are transmitting
is only between me and them
You would think it is of love, joy or just mundane needs

The sky and the birds are saying but
the one and the same
The plentiful and the barren are saying but
the one and the same
The flower and stone are saying but
the one and the same
All life, the moving and the unmoving are saying but
the one and the same.

O Shambho! how to make the fools know:
You are but only me

Of Shiva and Me

Shiva and me have built
an immense fire together

We keep each other
happy and warm

A million more
could enjoy this warmth

Shall we build a sacred space
so all shall know this warmth

Dhyanalinga

If the fruits upon the tree
were invisible, how many
would sense the sweetness
to know the lush nourishment.

Been trying to paint your
fruits in bright hues to make
even sightless to see.
But they challenge me with
not just sightlessness but
senselessness too

The Miracle that you are goes in vain.
The tower of light that
you are goes unseen and
Your Immense Power unfelt.
All busy in their dung heads.

Was not just willing to shed
my life but willing to give up on
other lives dear to my Heart to see you here.

I wait for more sensitive ones
to come by or slumbering ones
to Come Awake.

Senseless

This eternal mischief
that these elements five did make
What a simple trap you set
to see no man can ever know rest
to struggle in seemingly endless unrest

The devil in you did decorate this trap
with sweet complexities of senses five
Senses and senses meet to leave one
senseless of all that is true

The door that blocks
is also the door that liberates
Which side of the door you are
is all there is

Shambho, my doughtiness and your grace
got me to your side of the door
If you are too choosy
as to who should cross this door,
a mistake with me you made

This new sense has left me so senseless
that I will keep this door open for
every vermin that can crawl and cross
Pardon me my treacherous arrogance
As I am only you

a feud with you

I fancied to divert the
attention from the pain in my Heart
to the pangs of Hunger
But alas the pain is too deep
that I am oblivious of those pangs if any.
Denied of its sap the body seems weak.
But it does not dull the pain a wee bit.
Hey Shiva I set up a grand
Celebration for you and what do you
do to me? If this journey is from
Moha to Moksha, you know I don't need
your help. Isn't it coming
too soon? Now I have a feud with
you. You will miss the celebrations
You rogue does that bother you.

Kalabhairava

Thunderous roar of Creation
Resounding Stillness of the Beyond.
Reside within for all to decipher.

In knowing the distinction
Does liberation exist
In access of this Chasm
Does One become Divine

In merging with this Timeless
Does One become the Source
The Source shall know Creation
in abandon and without Burden
Burden of life that leaves
many with a bent back
Shall leave you untouched
Beyond the phenomenon of Time and Space

Adi Guru

Ascetics distance
The stoic stance

All this they bore
And He could not ignore

Seekers so intense
Broke his obstinate stance

Celestial sages seven
Strived not in search of Heaven

But to find a way for every human
To find a way beyond hell and heaven

They toiled for their race
He could not withhold his Grace

He turned his sacred face
To south to look upon their race

They not only beheld his divine face
But held the downpour of ultimate Grace

As the Beginningless One flowed
In knowing, seven sages overflowed

To release the world
From its crusted mold

To this day the sacred knowing flows
We will not rest until every vermin knows

Adi Yogi

A quiet Sea
A quiet Day
A quiet Mind

But a raging Heart
Blazing with Fire
Of an ancient Sage.

Burning for many a millennia
Destructive for the ignorant
Enlightening for the seeking
Brutal to the stubborn
Tender to the willing.

When all the tricks fall
The First Yogi's Fire shall
Burn the ignorant pall
To light the future's citadel

Citadels of future are first
built in the minds of Ignorance or Light

These citadels when lit with Grace
Of the Blue-Bodied Maker of all race

Will be a worthy place to dwell here
and a passage to the ways of the beyond.

O' how fortunate are we
To carry the Fire of the Adi Yogi.

Blue Net

Nets are of many sorts
Some to trap Fish or Birds
To snare a Hare or to hold Hair
Many nets of capture and kill
But the Yogi casts his net
that is both of Light and Darkness
A Cosmic Net that breathes both
Life and Death like they are One.
I for one have been in this
Cosmic Blue Net by choice
or so I would like to think
This is not a trap but a release
from puny nets of shame and fame
of friends and foe. Of love and hate
of familiar and unfamiliar
Now shamelessly casting the net
for all to deliver them to Him
My lord of the Blue Net

Presage for the Petty

Can assumed sanctity
of birth be a qualification
Can scholarship in dead
scriptures make one know
Can sheer manipulation of
Market like popularity touch Him
To know Adiyogi you at the
least be a Yogi. Obliteration
of the boundaries of individual
nature the only way.
O' knowledgeable ones
Just know – He loves the
Borderless Ignorance.

Eternal

In amplified crescendo of Shiva
Did I find the peace of the eternal
The stillness of the internal
Dissolved the turmoil of the external

The vastness of the dance external
Is puny in this boundless internal
If you dare to dissolve the external
It is all internal
It is eternal

Fatal Fragrance

The smell of Shiva
Set me upon treacherous
but an eternal path

Just a Snort
I was done

Eternal Stuff
Fatal to oneself

Smell of Shiva

The silent Mountains
Stoic but full of eyes
The roaring river-rapid
in a hurry to lose itself

A nameless valley steeped
in occult ways. People as
Earthy as earthworms
Found ways to bend nature
to their will, seeking the
mundane through magic

The smell of Shiva
makes me set down
for a night, a day and a night
Now how to tell the fools of
His plumbless ways.

—— ••••• ——

Stillness of the rocks
are utmost comfort to the
Still One. Stillness of the
within is no rock, but for
sure Rocks.

—— ••••• ——

It is tenderness that the tiny
being needs
But cruelty is what Shambho decrees
– beyond sanity
Strange are his ways but no stranger
is He to me
Cruel or Insane I am only for Him.

Of Shiva

One who has
Denied oneself
Of oneself.
Will talk of love.

What is love
To a being
Who belongs
Not to himself
But to Him.

Shiva

In this genderless scape does play
All that is this and that
Him and her, you and me
Don't miss the canvas
In the play of multiple hues

Shambho

The flying bird
the crawling worm
Are faces of same norm
though of different form

The early bird makes its life
the early worm meets its death
Is this life's cruel norm
you missing life's charm

Life and death are but one realm
Heaven and hell a conceited sham

Don't you fade your life in futile race
Heed to the wisdom of boundless Grace

Shambho

Profoundly alone

Blessed with keenness
of attention, life happened
in abundance. Smallest happenings
were immense, as after all
an Atom could be a Cosmos. All
a game of perception. As my
many lives unfolded, life
pitched up to be a torrent.
Rich and Vivid but no Small
or Big. All was thrown at me.
Flowers and Filth. Offered
sweetest of Love and Devotion
and vilest of treachery and abuse.
Regarded by the Reputed and
Rubbished by the Rascals. All
that can be and cannot be
has been mine but untouched am I.

Alone, as even Shiva has abandoned
me from being a companion
As even He has become One with
Me to leave me Profoundly Alone.

EPIC

Mahabharat

There is no other story
but of brothers and sisters
of wives and husbands
of teachers and disciples
of friends and enemies
of wealth and power
of love and treachery
of life and death
Like all stories
But for the One
Conscious One.

Dharma Adharma

Dharma Adharma is not of right and wrong
Nor of good and bad
But of what leads one towards truth or untruth
Dharma Adharma is not limited to code of conduct
For a king, priest or the citizenry
But an eternal law that will allow transcendence from all that is
Learning to use life as a stairway to the Divine

For Krishna

O' the blue-bodied cowherd
Ever playful in love and war
Says "Does not matter who you love or kill"
Playful, ever so playful
Don't you let yourself be deceived
And fail to see
The immensity of his wisdom and light
The buccaneer of love and war
O' the blue-bodied one
None ever before or since
So playful in love and war

Blue

As I come awake to the peacock Call
Blue it sounds in my ears,
I open my eyes and look at the ceiling
It has become like the open sky all Blue
The floor being my choice has always been Blue
Oh! look my tongue Blue, Blue, Blue...
If I bleed I am sure it will be Blue
O' Keshava the White Mountain
Has turned Blue too.
Or is it the depth of my passion
For you Neela Megha that
Has turned my vision Blue.
Is this the result of
Your blatant invasion of my every pore.
Is this your way of revealing to the World
How shamelessly I long for you.
Now that there is no hiding
That I am mad with your Blue
And I live in you
And you live in me, my Blue.
Now that my inner color has leaked into the world
There is no escape for you my Blue.

Vyasa

A scoundrel is knowledgeable
A fool will know.
A sage is an empty page.

Yudhisthira

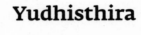

A good man
a good man
And a good man.

As tedious as
Only good can get.

But when life gets mean
You will want a good man.

Panchali

So full of fire she had to be of fire.
Of passion pride shame and rage.

Too fiery to rise, too fiery to fall.
Her beauty and passion consumed all.

What a lovely snare.

Arjuna

Unwavering aim
Turns into a mean game
The quiet warrior a deadly force
Strong of body and mind
Weak of vanity and whim
Enjoined with god because
Destiny's tool but nobody's fool
A Man, A Man, Oh Man.

Karna

Karmic burden of
Lives forgotten
Make him mean
By things unseen.

A good man
Who is no good.
A great being
Only when he stops being.

A fate's child
Best untouched.

Bhima

Born of the wind
A restless force to reckon with

Can be led by a mountain or a hill
a valley or a mole

Can make the oceans rise and roar
but cannot even lift a pebble

The loveable bubble

Megha

The dark mystic of the ages
arrives not with a bundle of messages
But with mischief that enamors kings and sages
Determined to have his way with a smile
he did commit ravish deceit and slaughter even
Life does not absolve him of taint
but could not bind him even a moment
He's no saint or sage
but glowed with wisdom for all ages

Isha

The mountain peaks that haunted me from my infancy
At their feet now I set you down

Many a seeker's deep longing
impelled me to set a part of me
at the foothills of these sacred mountains
these mountains where seers and sages walked

The most glorious one, my light and liberation,
chose these magnificent peaks to dissolve

Now at their feet, a sturdy band of seekers are
pursuing the timeless, immortal path

Their seeking and longing, their struggle and joy,
their pain and love, I bear in my heart

These wondrous creatures, these Ishas,
sure shall bring light to the world

Isha USA

A mother has to bear much pain
To nurture and deliver a mortal swain
Still willing to bear the pain
As the joys of breaking the limits
Of this coil no one can explain

And now to build the spiritual womb
That will render the mortal beyond the binding coil

To be on this earth and not to be of it
To open an inward eye that will
raise one beyond the fleshy bond
To render the mortal coil into an immortal key

Persevere in expectant joy
like a pregnant Mother.

I am in you

O' ISHAS

You never know how big and tall you are
Till you are asked to rise
If you are true to my will
You will stand tall like the Himalayan peak

The divine you seek
Will play in every step that you take
May you rise and show the world
What it means to be a ISHA
O' ISHAS, I am in you,
to make the Divine a daily happening.

Be Isha

How can you be Isha?
That which rules the Universe is Isha
The intelligence that crafted this creation is Isha
The very cosmic space is Isha
The worm that crawls is Isha
The leaf green or brown is Isha
The earth and the sky are Isha
All that is, is Isha
All that is not is Isha
How can you not be Isha

PEOPLE
and PLACES

An Ode to a Beautiful City

Crafty hands and loving hearts
extract beauty of stones
and earth. The magic of
human ingenuity competes
with the Divine Prowess
to create.
No, no. Isn't it the
Best Compliment for the
Divine Hand. A micro organism
in this limitless cosmic space
can even feign the Divine.
O' We the homosapiens are a mean
lot, of all the mess we make
a few things we do get right.
No mean feat.

Kashi

Domes and towers of stone and metal
Palaces and parliaments for pleasure and
purpose. Schools and temples for pursuits
of here and beyond, all these and more
make a city that people build.

But a city with a tower of light
and cremation ghats that burn eternally
with only aspiration to dissolve.
Where Death is sacred beyond life.

A city built for Death and Dissolution
where life happens with
the knowledge that there is no tomorrow.

A tower of light that lights up
not only all that there IS, but also
That which is Not – Shiva

Kashi

A tower of light of immeasurable height
The cosmic reach of the blessed city drew
men of all kinds. Craftsmen and tradesmen
scholars and priests, merchants and mendicants
builders and boatsmen. Seekers of every kind
flocked to suck at the teat of eternity.
Mother Ganga took an odd turn to embrace
this sacred space. Even ensnared the Great Lord
Shambho by its charm.

The great Kashi lost in the folds of human memory
Now left graceless by the invading hordes
and the callous kind who administer bereft of
the sacred touch, but of greed and indolence
of the worst sort.

May blessed Kashi rise again
And touch one and all with its
Sacred light

Kampuchea

Of tuk-tuks and temples
Of massage parlors and marsh lands
Of paddy fields and prawn soups
Of childlike adults and children who lost theirs

If you are up for a barbeque
choose a snake or a crocodile
or an ostrich or would you like
a kangaroo? Or if you have
more cannibalistic tastes
you are in fact a bit late, you
missed Mr. Pol Pot.

A gentle culture surrendered
its all to a despot
Brought down from the dizzy
pride of building Angkor to
the despicable state of selling children.

Dear Kampuchea, your time
has come to rise again, not in fury
but to your natural gentle Glory.

Angkor

In devotion or fear
Or just ambition for power
in here and hereafter
An incredible effort
of the stony sort

Human genius powered by
the indomitable devotion
Touched a dimension
that one has to concede is Divine

The magnificent face
of the God for whom they toiled
Was bludgeoned and erased
By the fervor of faith
of a different kind

Though the footprint
of the Original One haunts
you in every nook
All the effort has come to ruin

Bhaktapur

Meticulous brick work
ancient dreams of a monarch
A platform for divine dance
they did not spare a single nuance
In their efforts to decorate and enhance
this divine town of devotion and penance
Streets and alleys in great beauty flow
in manifest of the devotees' inner glow
An edifice for the richness of human heart
In not knowing this, your life is yet to start.

Bhaktapur (Nepal)

Culture so gentle
Under mass of time did crumble
In an effort for eternal mantle
They made every step a Temple

Nepal

Just a place to smoke and sip
An organized place to gossip
A society steeped in Devotion and Relaxation
Devoid of need to travel, lived life in grand fashion

HOME AT HUMDE

The valley floor of Humde
seems like Home to me who
is being drawn to these less
travelled trails among these
spectacular Mountain peaks.
Ever since he invaded my
Breath and Being and drew
Me into his cosmic Breast
I am like an infant in the
comfort of a loving Mother's
womb. Not a care about life
or Death. Unfettered even by
longings of the Beyond as
Here has become Beyond and
Beyond is Here.

Yalbang

The rugged mountain peak
Looks down upon me like
an ageless visage of frozen
Wisdom, cast in stone but ever changing
What immortal hand or eye could
mold these masterpieces of
Imperfections. For those who
have surrendered to the comforts
of plains, harshness of the mountain
scape is inhospitable at the
least. The terrifying prospects of
Mountain scape is for the ascetic kind
Divorced from the pleasures of life

But once you are into the
Madness of the mountains
The lure that drew not just
Explorers and adventurists but
wisest of the sages and mystics

As being in the labyrinth of
Mountains and the consequent valleys
Is closest to being back into
The womb of life making source

Madness, Magic, Miracles all possible
In the Mountains

Tibet

The forlorn notes of the flute
Echoing off the mountains in stony suits

Though they are as much life as man or beast
They stoic stand, mute to cries of human heart

The stoic peaks no more reverberate
With vibrant chants or forlorn flute

But the remorseless and lust insatiate
Throb of engines and cruel sounds of machine grate

Stern uniform, sterner eyes – rifles ready to speak
The gentle people taken but with a squeak

Tibet

The greens
The blues
The snow whites
The sandy browns
Coppers and Cobalt
Endless mountains
stoic in stance

Moods played out in
their halo of clouds
Moods of melancholy and joy

These ever changing moods
adorned by numberless rainbows
The profound past
The eager youth

A tiger tamed
A leap of a few centuries
Needs a leap of faith

In its throes of change
May dear Tibet gain

Hayman Isles

A mountain sunk and dwarfed
In an oceanic aggression
Transformed those proud peaks
Into a string of these pearl isles
A thousand shades of blue
Merge the two incomprehensible
Blues of ocean & sky
As if confused by this mingling
A few birds are diving in
and some fish are making an attempt to fly
Hey man! Did you know the whales
are climbing mountains
The salty reach of these waters
Has brought floating vessels
And waving palms to their mountain peaks

These half drowned mountains
Have become joy and pleasure of
Exceptional beauty and grace

Athens

The city of goddess Athena
who fed herself upon the
cerebral mush. Placed wisdom
upon the highest perch.
A land that honors knowing
and wisdom as the loftiest
must have a lesson or two
for those who worship muscle,
money and meanness.
When military machines and
the economic Bull ravages the
landscape and the mindscape
brute and not beauty of the
human nature will be the victor.
Greeks built grand edifices
for wisdom, love and
the sheer pleasure of living
only to be ravaged by forces
of pillage to establish dogma
and blindness to cast a
shadow of ignorance upon
these children of wisdom
and knowing. May Athena
rise again in the cerebral
mush of every man and
wisdom find its highground.

CONSUMMATION

As I sit here upon the
snout of land jutting
into the Arabian sea
boiling in a stormy mood
The moods of an ocean
are alluring from the safety
of the landed vantage.
Seafarers would have a different story to tell
like the spectator and the sportsperson
All the thrills and spills that one
enjoys has a price, that someone pays
leaving the puny human struggles of
deluge, drainage, or even drowning.
The spectacular beauty of Monsoon
fury is without parallel.

Let us look beyond our struggles
and feel the fulfilment of the
parched land and all other
life being consummated in a
wild and wonderful way

My Grief

These blood-soaked mountains of Lebon
pretending innocence
covered in the raiment of spring blossom
and the earthy smells and flowery fragrances.

Striving to cover the shrieks of the terror-stricken
freshly made widow
and the incoherent cries of the babe in her arms,
the cool breeze from the Mediterranean toils
to cover the nostrils with a salty camouflage

The stench of fear, pain, death and grief
linger on to soak one's heart in despondent grief
of wastefulness of life and death

Standing beyond life and death, still
by choice a part of it
I let this seamless grief sink in

Having witnessed the murder of love,
trust and the fundamentals of humanity
in the painful knowing that elements
more precious than life can die

This seamless grief I make my cloak
to contrast my blissful core

The Dead Sea

A sea that you cannot even drown in
It takes life even to take life
Only in constant transaction
Even the possibility of cosmic action

The sea that got walled in
Cannot host even a wandering jinn

To soak in this mineral soup
Is like being in the motherly sap
The salty sap of the earth
Life nourishing but named Death

Zenobia

Zenobia, the royal Amazon
burned with ambition to reach the horizon

Where her strength failed
her guile did prevail

The spirit that had many a man conquered
succumbed to the only frailty of womanhood

She set fear in the heart of a Caesar
but was felled by the heart of a senator

So full of fire and venom
but tamed by hearth and home.

The life that queen Zenobia did live
keeping account of the times – hard to believe

Read your history

Palmyra

The harsh lands
did not stymie their hands
The terrain that gods abandoned
man found reason to be reclaimed
The merciless land he adorned
with temples, palaces and abode
Traders crisscrossed
mulling stories told and untold
Risking death if waylaid
or to be taxed for all that they carried
If the toll did not spell doom
the exotic whore did well to damn

The proud columns and towers stood to tell the story
of passion and kindness, of love and lust, of greed and treachery
life and death, blood and gore, and a stony Glory.

Being in Damascus is like reliving
an ancient connection of guts, greed,
trade, adventure and of course the
longing to know and share.

Africa

The dark continent –
a fair ground for all men
to commit abominable dark deeds

Fertile land soaked in blood
Unprejudiced as to who should die
they slaughter all – man, woman or child
renders the soil rich, blood-soaked

Lives of beast and man tangled
as the land yields the dark oil
seems like the oozing of the bloody soil

One leads to another
bringing in men with hearts
harder than the hardest stone they seek

This not about death of raging glory
just earth sucking back her soil
enriched not just by flesh and blood, but the soul

As we play our games, a continent lies stranded
the dignity of this humanity, crushed and mangled

America

The brooding darkness of these woods
fed upon the native blood
In the twisted tangle of the fallen wood
the spirit of the fallen Indian stood

O brothers, your identity a mistake
those who oceans crossed did make
The greed for gold and land laid waste
the spirit of wisdom and grace

The children of those, who by murder did take,
are taintless of their forefathers mistake
But those who lived, fed upon the milk of courage and pride,
stand as spirits of defeat and shame

O the murdered and the murderous
Embrace me. Let me set your spirits to rest

To the uncreated

Hurtling through the California space
gentle dunes of undulating schemes
For which the creator found such express need
melted rock to craft these heedless dreams
Now suited in summers browns
dotted with buttons of green crowns

So inviting these rolling schemes
compelling me to set my feet free
As I walk this much fondled land
come upon breaks in the smooth brown wrap
The painful songs of the melted rock
that froze in poses of the uncreated

Like the aborted babe of the unwed mother
lay in throes of the agony of the uncreated
Monumenting the pain of human heart
of both loved and unloved sort

Me stand like a mossy rock
beyond all, like the eternal stock
I could be a balm to every heart
or a psalm that you sang and forgot.

To Trees in Tennessee

O' Blessed Beings
Your green raiment
source of our breath and being
Your stoic stance
mistaken for lifeless existence
Your immense presence
could escape human sense

This lack of cognizance
could mean a disastrous consequence
But for now you and me
in this intimate embrace
The joy of sharing each other's breath
is beyond the joy of having a breathless wench
I can only nourish you with tears of gratitude
When I come back in winter
you will stand naked and gray
Giving a taste of what the world would be
without you being gay

You, a permanent resident
Me, a wandering vagabond
But can I ever break my breath bond?
Wait till I am done with my deeds
I will lie at your roots to nourish you with my body's juice
To become the sap of your sap
To put back all that is Hers into Her lap
Till then you and me in this romantic romp
Lest someone should notice
Let us carry it on without any pomp

NY

As the Hudson flows
in its ever tranquil mode
The Sirens scream, Yellow devils
screech, Subway thunders, drains express
their nasty nature, flying machines keep
roaring by at regular intervals and Anxious
faced people are going about with the
certainty of Death. The city lives as
life passes by

When your lifestyle matters
more than your Life – Anxiety is Natural.

Manhattan

Like termite mounds
these dwellings of humans rise
Everyone of his own purpose
lives and walks this busy maze
Many a good man has lived and died
held in the spell of this dizzy haze
The lure of the maze
transcends all class and grade

The prostitute and the saint
the musician and the actor
and of course the slick businessman,
all come to do their own trade

If you walk a mile, you can smell it all
the stench of
prosperity and poverty
food and filth
sin and sainthood
life and death

JAPANI

If you are not a *japani*
for sure your car could be
if not, your television is
if not, your motorcycle definitely is
at least check your phone
or maybe the stereo. Ah, now
your footwear-*joothi*. That is it.

You may never have been to japan
no matter where you live, japan
has entered your life.

These gentle people, so unassuming,
humble and delicate in stature
and conduct. How do they manage
to invade everyone's lives.

Their stoic silence is not of the
weak, their gentleness for sure
not weakness. Determined, Dogged
and Dignified. They stand in
Silent Strength.

Deutschland

Guttural gumption
of the German tribe
Epitome of discipline,
the very mechanics of skill
Even the wily English
took a deutsche queen

But the German dream
lies waste consequent
to one man's wanton
acts of unparalleled tyranny

May the world not breed
another one of his kind
Never, Ever, Never.

Español

The women have to stomp
unlike the gentle flamingo
as the men's hearts are lost
to football or the raging bull.
Here even if you are just another
Salvador, the heart is of a Matador.
Spaniard sans adventure and danger
is like the sunken treasures of yore.
The mountains, the beaches, the food
above all their passion – ¡Fantástico!

English

A land that inspired
silken bards in hordes

Ancient tongues lost their
battles against this celtic flair

Sons of this cold but pretty isle
in conquest have outdone Alexander's guile

Viking, Roman, German assault
revisited this isle but conquered it not

Not lacking in ingenuity or cunning
went on in rampage and compassion winning

Though conquered lands would in
control remain not as times did the armies in

What the majesty's much prided armies could not win
Minds and hearts in multitude fair language did win

Goa

Cool sands
Warm sea
Green hills
Gentle people
No heaven this
But must confess
One may forget
The need for heaven

Do not crowd it
Do not dig it
Do not scar it
Just leave it
Coming generations
Need to know the
World was beautiful

Let us not work the land
Let us work upon ourselves

There is a heaven within
Scar not ambience without.

BHARATVARSH

Hmm, an assembly of leading
lights. Make more sound
than light. Making light
of grave issues and gravity
to inflated selves. Seems
like they are in favour of
volume rather than wisdom.
After a torturous grind
a semblance of sense.

A time has come for a new
beginning to inspire and
nurture the ailing glory.
Glorious as it was has
lost its sheen and verve.
Sabotaged from outside,
sodomised from within.
A time has come to rejuvenate
and restate. Who we have been
Who we are and Who we want to be.

Hindustan

An ancient land
Where Man learned to excel
Without having to propel
himself away from the
Principles that maketh
life process and the universe

A land where man was not
eager to do his own will
but to fulfill the will of the divine

He grew in knowing and learning
to enhance himself into an
exuberance of intelligence and emotion
Enshrined the carnal and the divine
Delved deep into the innards
of creation, deciphered the primordial
mastered the melody and the math
of music of sound and all its
manifestations. Above all
found the doors of freedom
Assured of final freedom
Came to an ease and beauty
Where life was not burden but
a Bounty. A copious production
of effulgent and gentle beings
occurred. Masculine and feminine
found their fulfillment and
went Beyond. An ideal prey
for the brutal forces from
across.........

Tamil

Dusty step and muggy heat
Idli sambar is all that you can eat
Lusty people in these temples and towns
Pushing and pulling melting in sweat
There are as many shades of summers here
As there are variety of chutneys to savor
Though the odors of sweat and breath
Is not something that you can relish
The sweetness of their hearts' fragrance draws you here
The dark gusty people may not be an impressive stature
But even the Divine Ram in despondence
Sought help and succor from this lot
This seemingly hapless but gusty lot
Have completely stolen my heart
Their unfailing trust and spiritual lust
Choicelessly made me manifest
the Guru's dream in their midst.

India

She wore a raiment
of so many a hue
An unfamiliar eye would think
she is madness true
Her children are such
multi-flavored stew
This amalgamation of culture:
a heady brew

Isn't man just an outcrop
of the land that his forefathers slew
Its antiquated history
of blood and beauty knew
A faraway visitor here saw
what man or god could ever do
Now it is time that you and me
blow life and breath anew

GRACE

Dance

When joy fills your Heart
Even your bony, clunky
limbs become graceful.

All creatures when at their
Best burst forth into Dance.
Not just the graceful
King Cobra or a delightful
Peacock. Even gangly
Cricket and ungainly
Hippopotamus do their own gig.

In this land even Gods,
Sages and Seers dropped
falsehood of serious dignity
and Danced to their hearts content

Make life a Dance of Grace

My Smile

As the snow fell in heaps
water froze and life stood
still. I walk out to
see how life is faring
without heated rooms
or woolens. All was well
just a bit circumspect
in expression. As I felt
the freeze creeping up from
the ends of the body, a smile
spreads upon my face
as my smile is one thing
that weather cannot freeze.
You will have to burn it
down upon the pyre.

Glory

Sun rose
and
Sun set

Celestial objects unmasked
and
masked again

The world is clothed
and
unclothed

Bodied
and
disembodied

The glory is on

Drums of Destiny

As the Drums work out
their earth-shaking beat
Not just to augment the beat of the heart
But to let the song of life sing in full throttle

Full throated
Full blooded
Full hearted
Is it not the way life should be
To make it as full as it can be
To shake the limited to quake
and crumble into the limitless sea
of all that we are not but it is all
that we are. The vast emptiness
of eternal void, the blissfulness
of falling into a bottomless pit.
Untouched by the surface of life
but soaked in the very lap of life.

When you hear the Drum
It is not of just sound 'dumb.'
It is the call of your Ultimate Destiny.

———•••••———

Flight is only for birds and angels
So said the dogmatic rascals.
Of course they didn't count the spirited humans
Who shook off both gods and demons.

———•••••———

Exuberance of life
Neither has age nor time

In savouring a slice of life
there is divine delight.

———•••••———

Meditation Halls and Motorcycles
All a consequence of Grace
One of Man and another of the Divine

Just Playing...

There are private spaces
in my mind where I agree
with all and sundry. But
there are public spaces in my
mind where I could debate
all that anyone says or thinks.
This is not a Contradictory
Existence, just that deep down
I never took sides of any sort.
Though I stand stoutly for all
that I take up. Don't you go
thinking I am in a confessional mode
Just playing with you, as deep
down in this me there is really
no you and me. Just playing...

Become Me

I was born in my mother's womb
but she did not create me
I eat the salt of this earth
but I do not belong to her

It is through this body that I walk
but I am not it
It is my mind through which I work
but it could not contain me

In the limitations of time and space I live
but it has not denied me
unboundedness

I was born like you, I eat like you,
sleep like you, and I will die like you
but the limited has not limited me,
life's bondages have not bound me

As the dance of life progresses,
this space, this unboundedness,
has become unbearably sweet

Become love and reach out
Become me

Transactions of Life

As trees take on many hues
A Colourful Celebration of the
Coming death. As Colourful
leaf floats down to impregnate
the earth that is only reclaiming
the nourishment that infused into
the tree. The transactions of life
and death. A continuum of cycles
of the physical world. When done
with the exuberance of life gives
One a sense of joy. When bereft
of the needed exuberance and lassitude
takes on to become a morbid
depressive death. Let the leaf
fall. To fall willingly when it
is time is Grace. Know the Grace
of fall time. And it is not about
the Colourful leaf but of Life.

Kattu Poo (Forest Flower)

The flower is wild
Fragrance not so mild
Spreads its Blissfull Grace
This Bliss can flood Human Race
To know our eternal Space
So all will live in Grace.

Weaves of Grace

As a Weaver strives to put
one thread upon another
Every thread as crucial
as the other, for bare threads
to evolve into graceful fabric.

So is life my Beloved
Every thread as crucial
as the one before and after.
Weave you should the threads
of life of complex texture and hue
into a fabric of beauty and grace
fit for the boundless Being – Divine

Fabric not just a device to
cover the body of parts private.
Fabric that shall allow you to
touch the organic beauty of
Creation and become a passage
to privacy to cohabit the
Inner Divine. Threads of
love, threads of prudence, threads of
play and threads of work
Threads of closeness and distance
Threads soaked in sanity of
Sense and insanity of Bliss

Threads of such varied texture
and hue, to weave it all into
One graceful Garment.
Devotion my Beloved the
only way. Ungraced
by Devotion it can all
turn into messy knots.

Make life a weave of Grace
My Beloved

Dance

When your Heart if full
And Mind unmindful as
to who you are or not

Your Feet shall Dance
There is no method but an
Abandon

———·····———

Playfull...

If you want your life to be playful,
you need a heart full of love,
a joyful mind, and a vibrant body.

Life is a Play for one who is
absolute Balance.

A View

If you strive to climb
beyond the petty pits
of your thoughts and emotions
If you strive to leapfrog
over the pits of prejudice,
peaks of anger, chasms of
fear, cesspools of hatred
and death-traps of frustration,
despondence and depression.
You shall rise to a perch with
a View. Where you could relish
the endless fields of rich blossoms
of love, joy, bliss
and peaks of ecstasy.
Open your mind for a life
with a View

Traitor Within

Fortresses can protect not
fragile well being of the know nots

Outside enemy you can vanquish
with fortresses and armies of your wish

The traitor within cannot be demolished
unless you touch the grace of the Realized

Even deadwood can become fiery light
if only touched by the flamy sprite

A source that can quench and make lives bright
to set the tangled spirits to ultimate flight.

me And ME

The impish me
and the absolute ME

Many think a contradiction
but a perfect complement

My love, my joy, my laughter and my play,
but a façade to cover the absolute stillness that I am

My words and my songs, my smiles and my mirth
are but a ploy to entrap you in my limitless void

Both men and Gods were made in this void
O Beloved if you dare, come – dissolve

Dumbfounded

When the flower opened its
Petals and sprayed its fragrance
into the not so fragrant world,
dramatic as it was there was
no attendant music and there
was no adulatory applause.
So it is when the greatest of

Events happens within you.

Just Snort

The roots of Divine
are entrenched in this Body
Where the flowering of the Divine occurs
there Heaven Is.
This Divine flowering happens
not in the heavens above
but in the Inner Spaces.
None can see the Flowering
But can anyone miss the fragrance.
Just snort. You shall know.

Laugh your head off
If you can
Cry your heart out if you
cannot laugh
Know the abandon of
doing something where
You are not

If you are clueless and dumbfounded
about the nature of the profound
In playfulness I found the profound

Of Sweetness

The sacred sound
I refused to utter

The sacred space
I refused to enter

But you entered me unasked
through crevices unknown

Leaving me in sweet tremble
causing nameless, unspeakable ecstasies

Every pore, every cell
the very body a honey hive
of sweetness...

Me

As ordinary as ordinary can be
As special as special can be

Gentle fragrance of grace
Overwhelming power to brace

Taintless of virtue or sin
This sovereign and shameless Jinn

Appears to be an impossible ridge
But is a most accessible bridge

Cross you can to the beyond
If only willing to leave yourself behind.

Grace

We have found the flame
that can burn beneath the water

We have found the union
that can be united under the severest knife

We have found the bliss
that can bloom even in the very face of death

We have found the love
that can stir the most barren of hearts

We have found the guile
that can slip out of hell's own corner

We have found the grace
that has placed us beyond all disgrace

We have found a jointedness
that can make Shiva feel like two

O Shambho! Your grace brought us this far
May we proceed unto you

Fortune

Fortune is not found by
the diggers of gold or by those
who scavenge the marketplace

Fortune is not theirs who dive
into oceans to find what those
before them could afford to lose

In search of fortune, the pittance
that has enslaved too many lives
Bodies bent in search of fortune
Minds filled with madness of fortune
Souls enslaved in search of fortune
Lifetimes gone by in pursuit of fortune

It is in giving away what the slaves
of fortune value, One becomes fortunate

Fortunate are those who are blessed with giving
Fortunate are those who have lost need to hoard
Fortunate are those who do Shambho's bidding
Fortunate are those who mingle and merge in Him

Race

A Grim face
An endless race
At the market's pace
Life pulped by a mace
What a disgrace
To miss this Grace

Karma

Pattern so intricate
Enamors like moth to light

Drawn into this web
That offers protection and death

Death not as a onetime happening
But as a repetitive pattern

If you are oblivious to the
cramping suffocation

Feels safe as a living grave
In complete absence of inner grace

You cannot be without it
Oh, the safety of its limited orbit

Use this grace and break it
Or you are just lost, damn it

———•••••———

In a loving embrace
there is divine grace

———•••••———

Recognizing the Divine
in each other is the
most graceful way.

———•••••———

Even a crack of an opening
shall bring the light flooding
Keep aside your bashful farce
Me shall engulf you in Grace.

Island

You an island have become
An island large or small
But an island still
The stillness of the infinite will
Knocking on your door like a thrashing mill
But the robustness of your little pride
Could take you on an endless ride
You need to know it is just the hide
Peeling your own hide
Sure not an easy ride
Piece by piece if you tear
You will be unable to bear
Let this me get beneath your hide
In one piece it will fall by the side

Fall in step with my stride
For sure it will be an easy ride

Across

This boat of many holes,
the reckless sailor that I am
have set upon oceans vast

Plugging the holes with people's lives,
"I've hoisted the flag of hope
Can't let it sink, you see"

The sail is torn, the mast broken,
the rudder has gone asunder
This boat powered only by my longing to share

Navigated by the Grace of my deepest hidden love,
this rickety boat held together only by your heart strings
and still I say, "I'll see you across."

My Way

As ordinary as ordinary can be
as glorious as glory can be

A gentle presence like a flowery fragrance
but an overwhelming devastating power

Seemingly simple but a complex contradiction
an amalgamation of all that is life and death

Spreads as sweet sense of ecstasy in you
as the fear of being lost haunts you

Your body quakes in shameless ecstasy
mind struggles to find some dignity

In love or in awareness
In work or in sadhana

This me is only for you.

Isha Foundation

Founded by Sadhguru, Isha Foundation is a non-profit human service organization supported by over eleven million volunteers in over 300 centers worldwide. Recognizing the possibility of each person to empower another, Isha Foundation has created a massive movement that is dedicated to address all aspects of human wellbeing, without subscribing to any particular ideology, religion or race.

Isha is involved in several path-breaking outreach initiatives to enhance the quality of rural life in India through healthcare and disease prevention, community revitalization, women empowerment, the creation of sustainable livelihoods, and Yoga programs. Educational initiatives empower rural children with quality education, while ecological projects have initiated mass tree planting drives, creating a culture of care for the environment to keep this planet liveable for future generations.

Isha's unique approach in cultivating human potential has gained worldwide recognition and reflects in Isha Foundation's special consultative status with the Economic and Social Council (ECOSOC) of the United Nations.

The Foundation is headquartered at the Isha Yoga Center, at the base of the Velliangiri Mountains in southern India, and at the Isha Institute of Inner-sciences (iii) on the spectacular Cumberland Plateau in central Tennessee, USA.

isha.sadhguru.org
facebook.com/ishafoundation
twitter.com/ishaUSA
instagram.com/ishafoundation

ishaoutreach.org
twitter.com/ishafoundation
youtube.com/ishafoundation
instagram.com/isha_usa